Colin Everard has worked for over 40 years with developing countries as a technical cooperation practitioner. Subsequent to his retirement from Her Majesty's Overseas Civil Service he worked in the UN System, in the field of international civil aviation. His contribution to the development of safe civil aviation has been widely recognised and he is a recipient of the Gold Award of the International Civil Aviation Organization. He has been a Fellow of the Royal Aeronautical Society, a Fellow of the Chartered Institute of Management and a Fellow of the Chartered Institute of Purchasing and Supply. Colin Everard's career details have been selected for inclusion in a data bank which has been established in the Bodleian Library, Oxford University, for the use of scholars and researchers. This is his fourth book. He lives in Vienna.

Sir Boris Uvarov K.C.M.G. He published his landmark research work
Grasshoppers and Locusts *in 1926. Sir Boris subsequently became*
the director of the Anti-Locust Research Centre in London. Internationally,
he inspired entomological researchers to redouble their efforts to seek ways
to control the desert locust – Schistocerca gregaria.

Desert Locust Plagues

Controlling the Ancient Scourge

Colin Everard

BLOOMSBURY ACADEMIC
LONDON • NEW YORK • OXFORD • NEW DELHI • SYDNEY

BLOOMSBURY ACADEMIC
Bloomsbury Publishing Plc
50 Bedford Square, London, WC1B 3DP, UK
1385 Broadway, New York, NY 10018, USA
29 Earlsfort Terrace, Dublin 2, Ireland

BLOOMSBURY, BLOOMSBURY ACADEMIC and the Diana logo
are trademarks of Bloomsbury Publishing Plc

First published in Great Britain by I.B. Tauris 2019
Paperback edition published by Bloomsbury Academic 2021

ISBN: HB: 978-1-7883-1435-0
PB: 978-1-3502-0212-2
ePDF: 978-1-7867-3485-3
eBook: 978-1-7867-2485-4

Typeset by Riverside Publishing Solutions, Salisbury, Wiltshire, UK

To find out more about our authors and books visit
www.bloomsbury.com and sign up for our newsletters.

To my lovable, and loving, wife Emy

Contents

List of Illustrations

Images are the author's own, unless stated otherwise.

Foreword

By
Robert A. Cheke

Professor of Tropical Zoology
Natural Resources Institute
The University of Greenwich

Farmers dread the arrival of locusts into their crops, as a swarm can destroy whole fields of millet, sorghum, wheat, rice, fruit or whatever else takes their fancy, very quickly. There is a variety of locust species found in parts of the Americas, Africa, Australia, Europe, the Middle East and Asia, but none is feared as much as the desert locust *Schistocerca gregaria*. It has two subspecies: the nominate form *Schistocerca gregaria gregaria* and a lesser-known variety, *Schistocerca gregaria flaviventris*, which infests Namibia, the Republic of South Africa, Botswana and Angola and even reaches Ascension Island. This latter snippet of information gives a clue to the species' incredible propensity to long-distance migration: Insects blown off course have even crossed the Atlantic.

Swarms may descend as if from nowhere, having travelled many kilometres to reach the field that they have chosen to destroy. However, before this can happen they have to increase their numbers to an extent that they can change their 'phase', from that of solitary creatures behaving like ordinary grasshoppers to the gregarious hordes that form cohesive swarms, flying by day instead of by night and darkening the sky. So, if they can be found before they succeed in reaching the swarming condition, they can be killed in a pre-emptive strike. If this fails they have another Achilles heel, and that is their 'hopper' stage. After hatching they remain flightless for nearly two months, when they can be attacked on the ground. But to control them in this manner they have to be found first!

Search and destroy missions were part and parcel of the work of the Desert Locust Control (DLC), established by the British Army during World War II and maintained as a civilian operation afterwards. Meanwhile, research into the biology of the creatures, to develop means to forecast their movements and improve means to control them, was masterminded by Sir Boris Uvarov FRS, who ran the Anti-Locust Research Centre, an antecedent of the Centre for Overseas Pest Research, which I joined in 1976 and which was eventually absorbed within the Natural Resources Institute of the University of Greenwich.

Glib words about finding and destroying locusts can never do justice to what is entailed in the epic struggle of this extreme form of applied entomology. Deserts are harsh and unremittingly tough places to work in, especially in the midst of wars and civil conflicts, so dangers, both natural and man-made, abound. In Colin Everard's fascinating and entertaining account of his involvement with the DLC in the fight against the desert locust you will read accounts of daring exploits and how he managed to survive many a close call. But such is the lot of those involved in protecting crops; when actions prevent famine it is worth the risk. Colin's enthusiasm and dedication to this task jump at you from these pages.

When there is a famine today, it is broadcast to the world by the mass media, but no one hears when a plague of locusts has been stopped in its tracks. Colin is one of the unsung heroes responsible for stopping many a plague. In these pages you will find out how he did it, why it was far from easy and why it nearly cost him dear on more than one occasion. This book is an enthralling read and a salutary tale.

Acknowledgements

'No man is an island, entire of itself
…
Because I am involved in mankind.'
John Donne, 1624

I think it is never easy for the humble author to write his or her acknowledgements, simply because it is impossible to express the depth of one's feelings of gratitude. Nevertheless, acknowledgements of help and support must always be properly recorded.

Four hundred years ago, John Donne wrote that no man is an island; if he had lived today he would have included 'or woman' in his poem. Over the years, there have been many interpretations of Donne's famous poem. Perhaps because of the circumstances of my working life, my interpretation has remained consistent – we can do few things of real substance on our own – and if one tries to adopt the *prima donna* approach, then our initiatives are almost certainly doomed to fail.

In my working life I was at the peak of my competence (as an international civil servant) about 20 years after leaving the Desert Locust Control (DLC) at the age of 31; when I refer to competence, I mean that the qualities with which we are endowed are used to their optimum effect.

Sometimes I used to think that the more I knew and understood about a subject, the more I realised there were gaps in my knowledge; so I had to learn more. And I never initiated an action of significance without first consulting the specialists who could advise me with their knowledge on any given aspect of the subject in hand.

So it has been the case with this book. I am a generalist. Certainly, I learned a lot along the way. After living with desert locusts in all of their stages for ten years, inevitably I accumulated a store of first-hand knowledge about the locust and its devastating threat to mankind. But if I insist, as I always do in my writing, on correctness, then the need for authoritative advice and consultation becomes essential. It is in this context that I now embark on my heartfelt acknowledgements.

There are three human pillars who share a major responsibility in their valuable contributions to my book.

Dr Lester Crook is Senior History Editor at the publisher I.B.Tauris. This is my fourth book. Lester Crook will always be remembered by me as the only editor who showed *immediate* interest and enthusiasm for my writing. I acknowledge with deep gratitude his ready responsiveness, his experienced advice, and above all, that Lester Crook requested a change in the thrust of my work, so that now we have greater emphasis on what I call The Desert Locust Control Story, including (at Lester Crook's suggestion) an account of the present desert locust situation, 60 years on from my description of the period of our efforts to control the desert locust scourge in the 1950s.

Robert Cheke is Professor of Tropical Zoology at the University of Greenwich, Natural Resources Institute. At the behest of Professor Ben Bennett (a cheerfully dynamic and supportive man), Robert Cheke called me by telephone to offer his knowledge and time to checking the scientific information in the text of my manuscript. I sent Robert Cheke my manuscript, pointing to the scientific sections. Shortly afterwards I received his response, which included the following words, 'Despite your request for me not to do so, I have read all of your manuscript...'! From that point, Robert Cheke became an encyclopaedic resource on all aspects of the desert locust's behaviour. What greater gift of scientific knowledge could a generalist author receive? Apart from Robert Cheke's suggested amendments, he educated me concerning the *transient* stage of the desert locust. The detail of the behaviour of the transient locust which is now included in the text (as explained in the Epilogue), are the words of Robert Cheke, not mine. I owe inestimable gratitude to Robert Cheke. Through his scientific knowledge of the desert locust, he has transformed the scientific content of a generalist's text into a text which is scientifically authoritative.

Keith Cressman is the Senior Forecasting Officer of the Desert Locust Information and Early Warning Service provided by the Food and Agriculture Organization (FAO) in Rome. FAO is a specialised agency of the United Nations. As stated above Dr Lester Crook, after reviewing the first draft of my work, asked me to include a section covering the present desert locust situation. We live in a dynamic, fast-moving world, especially in terms of technological developments. Having left the world of desert locusts 60 years ago, how best could I meet this challenge? Knowing that FAO took over in 1962/3 the desert locust control work of the DLC, with the help of Robert Cheke, I made contact with Keith Cressman, a man of knowledge linked with action. Within 15 minutes, Keith Cressman had provided numerous documents relating to the spectacular technological developments in the field of desert locust control during the last 60 years. I have acknowledged Keith Cressman's contribution to my Epilogue in the text, and it is deeply appreciated (including his translation of the word *Hemistio* into current Somali!).

I wish to acknowledge the ready assistance of my daughter, Professor Andrea Everard, of the University of Delaware, in the United States. Her field is Information Technology. For two years, Andrea has kindly shown a constant readiness to be of assistance. Apart from proofreading my manuscript text at various stages, Andrea has often supported me in her field of IT. Overall, Andrea has provided me with a great deal of practical help, for which I would like to express my gratitude; for the author, a highly knowledgeable and responsive resource is always a comfort.

I would like to acknowledge the good advice of Michael Dwyer of Hurst Publications, who reviewed my manuscript and recommended me to Dr Lester Crook at I.B.Tauris. Also, I acknowledge with thanks the advice received from Chelsey Fox, of Fox and Howard Literary Agents. Although the agency was full to capacity, Chelsey Fox kindly offered sound, straightforward advice concerning an appropriate publisher for my manuscript.

Austrians like to use an English phrase (in English), which is 'Last but not least…' Yes, last but certainly not least, I would like to acknowledge the support and assistance of my wife Emy. The lot of one's wife when one's time is consumed by writing for hours on end needs understanding, to say the least. Five years before I had the privilege of meeting my wife, Emy had studied for her Special Honours Bachelor of Science degree in Zoology, at King's College, University of London. For her entrance to the university, Emy was asked to write an essay. Her chosen subject for her essay was – the desert locust! After our marriage Emy accompanied me for five years, in Somalia and East Africa, where I was endeavouring to play my part in combating the desert locust scourge.

I have been afforded strong support in my writing of this book; and I have been showered with kindness, for which I will remain eternally grateful. Yes indeed, as I have shown in these Acknowledgements, none of us can afford to be what John Donne calls an 'island'; yes, each of us is a part of humankind.

Introduction

On the night of 10 July 1944 a 13-year-old boy of Dulwich College in south London was sleeping peacefully in one of the school's boarding houses. He was suddenly awoken by a woman's firm voice. 'Wake up, Colin,' she said, 'Get dressed and go downstairs; wait by the front door. Now!' At Dulwich, one of the first rules we learnt was to obey authority, so, a little confused, I got up and dressed. By the time I was downstairs, I was getting some idea of what was happening. With the droning of aero engines, explosions in the distance and the deafeningly loud staccato bangs of Bofors anti-aircraft guns which seemed to be firing into the heavens from the road outside, little imagination was needed to realise what was going on. Another of Hitler's air raids was in progress. Only this time there was an important difference: The aircraft which were attacking London were pilotless. The flying bomb, the V1, had arrived on the scene.

Our group of about 30 boys was instructed to run from the boarding house to the first of three tuition blocks, which were linked by what were loosely called 'the cloisters'. On arrival, we would bed down in a vast cellar. As we left the house, an ear-splitting salvo from the Bofors roared over our heads. Semi-petrified, I did my best to keep up with the running boys, most of whom were older, bigger and stronger.

But my best was not good enough. Halfway to the destination, as the group ran across a large gravelled area, I felt an elbow; then I slipped and fell. Suddenly I was prone, alone in the sea of gravel. I tried to take in my new situation: I could just make out the silhouette of the Science Block. Apart from this, all was darkness.

The noise around me in the blackness was tremendous. Apart from the Bofors and the aero engines, there were thunderous explosions. As I got up to head for the first block, I heard the roar of an aero engine. It seemed to be flying straight at the college. I tried to run faster. Now I could see the outline of the block. Just then, the engine roar stopped. I raced to the cellar entrance. At that very moment I heard a whine which, within a few seconds, became an intensely loud swishing, almost screaming, sound.

Then it happened. As I closed the cellar door behind me, the V1 struck the corner of the Science Block. The side and corner of the building I had made out in the darkness were no more. The cellar, already dimly illuminated, was instantly plunged into darkness. At the same time, what had been dank air was replaced by dense, choking dust. Next to me a voice said, 'Open the door, boy.' I obeyed and groped my way outside. A tall boy asked, 'What is your name?' 'My name is Everard, Colin Everard.' I sensed I was talking to a prefect. Then the prefect said, 'You got to the cellar late. You got yourself inside just in time, didn't you? You just had a close call. Next time, don't be late. It could be too late!'

A few days later, I was attending a cricket practice. Again, we heard the engine of the V1 Doodlebug cut out. We threw ourselves on the ground and pressed our hands over our heads; and we felt our hearts pounding. After the terrifying swishing sound, there was a thunderous explosion. I heard a thud next to my head. It was a jagged piece of shrapnel. Before getting up, I touched it, which was not intelligent.

I burned the tips of two fingers. I stood up and looked around. There, standing in front of me, was the tall prefect I had first met in the dusty darkness by the cellar entrance. 'It's Everard, isn't it?' he asked, 'You will soon be getting used to your close calls!' He gave me a quizzical smile; then he walked away. And I carried on with my cricket practice.

About a week later, as I left a French period a note was handed to me. I should go back to my boarding house to see the Housemaster, Eric Parsley. He was waiting for me. 'Ah, Colin, you are just in time,' he said. 'Your father said he and your mother have had a spot of bother. That could be an English understatement.' The phone rang; it was my father. 'Hello, Colin. I just wanted to keep you up to date. A Doodlebug fell in our garden in the night. The whole corner was flattened. Your mother and I are alright. When we next see one another, I will tell you more. But there is not much point in you coming home for the weekend. It's best if you stay at school.' 'Oh,' I replied, 'So you don't want me to come?' My father showed understanding to a son who apparently had little understanding. 'Well, you see, Colin, we don't have a house any more. Thank goodness you weren't in your bed at home because with the blast your bed was sucked out of the window. Now your bed is lying in what was our garden, on top of our uprooted plum tree.'

The V1 flying bomb was superseded by the V2 rocket, a missile altogether much more powerful, and therefore destructive, than its predecessor. At Dulwich, sitting in an English period one day, we heard a horrendous, reverberating thud, and an instant later, after some noisy juddering of the high, nineteenth-century wooden window frames, the windows' glass shattered. Helpless, we watched fragmented glass sailing through the classroom; as the glass struck an object, it exploded into uncountable fragments. Then all was quiet – and the cowering pupils continued their class work as the chill, winter air swirled around them. By now, we were used to the horrors of war; they so often seemed to be sudden and unpredictable. The only constant in the picture of war which accompanied our daily lives was destruction, both material and spiritual.

I have related these anecdotes with a main purpose in mind. There are those in the world who consciously engage in an activity which may well involve danger. For example, a professional soldier is not surprised when he or she encounters danger; that is to say that before becoming a soldier, the danger element was considered and fully accepted. There are a number of other professions where a danger element is recognised and accepted.

Or again, there are those who call themselves 'Adventurers'. These are people who deliberately seek adventure, an activity which is sometimes accompanied by danger. Some 'Adventurers' even make a living by their exploits, usually by writing about their adventures.

But, like millions of others, I did not fall into this category. Throughout my professional career, I never consciously felt the need to consider the danger element in my work. And even when, as a young conscripted subaltern, I was confronted with danger, I had not by choice become involved in a dangerous situation; I was there because I had been conscripted to do my National Service, which in the United Kingdom at that time was mandatory.

So, looking back, as someone who never sought danger, I find it surprising that, over the years, I found myself in so many situations which, by their nature, were unexpectedly dangerous.

In any case, having survived, I felt that some true accounts of situations in which I found myself might be interesting, sometimes perhaps even entertaining, for some to read. Although some of these survival experiences might seem incredible, I must reassure the reader that the substance of these stories is absolutely true.

Above all, this book is about the desert locust and our efforts in the mid-twentieth century to control huge, ravenous invading swarms in the Horn of Africa. From Chapter 2 onwards, I have recounted how locust plagues were brought under control. The whole story, which is of far-reaching significance to so many Third World countries, deserves *pride of place* in the accounts which follow. In the big picture, my unsought adventures become a nothing in comparison with the achievement of controlling locust plagues, an achievement which resulted in sparing millions of people the horrors of hunger and starvation.

With the above in mind, although the chapters may be read at random, I would nevertheless recommend that they be read in sequence. If this approach is adopted then, from Chapter 2, the reader will benefit from following the development of measures to control the ravaging desert locust. To have overcome the problem of devastating locust plagues, a problem which had afflicted mankind since at least biblical times, was one of the great, albeit unsung, achievements of the twentieth century.

I would like to add a word about context; one should constantly be conscious of context. For example, if someone today decided to walk through parts of north–eastern Somalia, he or she could (and probably would) be regarded as foolhardy, in the sense that survival at the hands of murderous bands and piratical thugs would be unlikely.

But the situation in terms of security in the Horn Africa 50 or 60 years ago was totally different to the situation of today. I used to walk with my Somali colleagues, accompanied by burden camels, for weeks on end. My colleagues, whether Somali, Ethiopian or Kenyan, were usually a delight to work with and we functioned together as an excellent team albeit, for me at least, in unusual surroundings.

A positive factor with respect to one's personal security 50 or 60 years ago concerned the attitude to foreigners which one met in, for instance, the countries of Africa. The influence of so-called religious fanaticism, linked with the widespread and easy availability of arms, made itself felt only much later. This meant that, regardless of religion, an attitude of openness, tolerance and friendliness was the norm. For most of us, the world of the mid-twentieth century and the world of today were, as far as personal security was concerned, very different. In the text of my book, the reader will note that not one of my related dangerous experiences was caused by religious extremism or racial hatred.

En passant, when we recall the journeys and exploits of missionaries and explorers in Africa, such as David Livingstone or Sir Richard Burton in the mid-nineteenth century, it seems remarkable how little attention they needed to pay to their personal security. These men were respected, and in the case of Livingstone even loved, for what they were. When Livingstone died in the heart of Africa, his bearers and followers carried his corpse, sometimes through harsh terrain which was steaming in heat and humidity, back to the coast; yes, they loved him.

So please accompany me on my unsought adventures. Although one might gain an impression that each experience occurred hard on the heels of the last, this was certainly not the case; for most of the related experiences we are looking at a time-span of some 10 years.

During this period I was working as a member of a team which was dedicated to developing methods to control desert locust plagues; this problem, a problem which had become the scourge of many tropical countries since pre-biblical times, was largely overcome during the 1950s. I would mention that, apart from my adventures, I was able to lead a fulfilling work life, unaffected by danger.

The setting for six of the seven chapters is the Horn of Africa. The last takes place in eastern Kenya; from demographic and topographical viewpoints, this area is an extension of the semidesert conditions which exist to the north–east, in the Horn.

As I have stated, the accounts may be read in chronological sequence, or at random. For the sake of completeness of each chapter (each chapter tells a stand-alone story), a minor degree of repetition occurs in one or two chapters. I hope I may be forgiven for this unavoidable situation.

In a nutshell, I have related what might be termed 'The Desert Locust Control Story'. I hope you enjoy these experiences from an age which, for a European like myself at least, was unique and which has now passed into history, probably never to re-emerge.

1

An Uninvited Christmas Visitor

I am a product of World War II, which means that deep down I can never forget the horrors of war, not to mention the limitations of the wartime education system, when so many young men, including teachers, were conscripted for military service. For some youngsters there was also the trauma associated with being evacuated to a safer haven from dangerous wartime focal points such as London.

In early 1949, a little over four years after the cessation of hostilities, like most young men at that time I was conscripted to perform my National Service. Later in the year, as an 18-year-old commissioned officer of the British Army, I received word that I would be sent to the then Somaliland Protectorate to serve with the Somaliland Scouts, a successor force to the Somali Camel Corps. I would be accompanied by three or four recently commissioned officers of what were called regiments of the Home Counties; my regiment was the Royal Fusiliers.

In Somaliland – after a stint patrolling camel watering-holes to keep the peace between tribal factions who sometimes 'poached' the water of different clans, causing enmity or bloody clashes – I was recalled to the main town, Hargeisa, to receive new posting instructions. Shortly before Christmas at the end of 1949, I had the pleasure of meeting my fellow officers of the regiments of the Home Counties. I had just turned 19 years of age.

A few days before Christmas, our small group was chatting over a beer. I believe it was John Whitmore who made the point that Christmas was a time for families to get together. As single men we had little place in the Christmas picture. Even if we were to be invited by a family to celebrate Christmas with them, we might feel we were imposing on a family whom we hardly knew; we were rather like the proverbial square pegs.

So why not detach ourselves from the family-oriented Christmas scene in Hargeisa? There were plenty of areas outside Hargeisa where we could spend Christmas alone; surely we could successfully find a suitable spot which would welcome three young bachelor British officers?

Where should we go for a few days' leave? For most of us, our image of the Horn of Africa, of which Somaliland is very much an integral part, is of a desert or semidesert waste of sand. Our TV pictures of today, perhaps showing us the coastal areas where pirates and thugs make it their business to terrorise the maritime industry, certainly accurately convey or confirm this image; yes, the Horn of Africa is largely desert of sand or gypsum rock, an area inhabited by nomadic tribes whose people spend much of their lives in search of water and grazing for their livestock.

However, as with most generalisations, there are exceptions. And we found one of these – the Sheikh Pass. As strangers to the general area who had become accustomed to the semidesert conditions around us, it seemed incredible that the Sheikh Pass should exist at all. In fact, it is not unusual in countries which have a coastline that after a littoral of various widths has been crossed, the topography rises rapidly, and soon one finds oneself faced with an escarpment ascending abruptly to several thousand feet above sea level.

In northern Somaliland, the Sheikh Pass winds its way through a range of impressive mountains. At its highest point, the Pass has an elevation of about 5,400 feet above sea level (1,640 metres). So in contrast to desert wastes, the mountains support a wide range of flora and fauna. It was in such areas that, a century ago, large numbers of animals had made their habitat. In the early 1920s the records show that 2,000 leopards were shot in one year. It is said that, in the late 1920s, erosion of soil due to over-grazing accelerated, and areas which had been well endowed with vegetation were laid waste. Vast quantities of sand and dust enveloped what was left of good grazing tracts; this happened especially in the summer thanks to the *kharif* wind, which blows strongly for four months. In the late 1920s and early 1930s, large numbers of wild animals migrated southwards, many finding a new home in Kenya.

So now, just a day or two before Christmas, we had our getaway plan; and we were driving out of Hargeisa en route to Burao. We took a cook with us whose name was Abdi; we were also accompanied by a soldier (an *askari*) of the Somaliland Scouts. The town of Burao lies several hours' drive east of Hargeisa; we used a truck with a capacity of 15 hundredweight. From Burao, we would drive to the Sheikh Pass.

The drive to Burao followed the pattern to which we had become accustomed. The dirt and sand road followed its monotonous course through the arid, semidesert conditions. When the surface of the road sometimes became firmer, potholes would shock the chassis and springs of the truck, and we would bounce in unison. There is very little surface water to be seen in Somaliland and my recollection is that we saw none during our journey. However, some distance from Burao we were treated to a wonderful phenomenon. Before us we could see the town, with the lovely white walls of its houses, in a perfect mirage. The mirage seemed like an artist's canvas shimmering in the heat and humidity as though a veil had been cast over the town.

Having passed through Burao, we took the road northwards to the village of Sheikh. The road had risen steadily and now we found ourselves at a higher elevation. The semidesert landscape had been replaced by generally stony terrain; here and there were patches of heavy sand or clay in which large bushes or trees were growing healthily. The altogether livelier landscape seemed to represent a transition between the desert and the mountains which we would reach the following day. We found a guest house where we could stay for the night. We enjoyed the basic amenities inside the guest house, and outside we found the fresh, crisp air bracing.

The following day was Christmas Eve. Before leaving the village of Sheikh for the Pass, we briefly visited an acquaintance we had once met in Hargeisa. He was a dapper, sporty education officer who lived with his family in Sheikh. After a brief chat and a drink to wish us all a Happy Christmas, we said goodbye. As our host showed us to the door he spotted our *askari*. He smiled and said, 'Good idea! It's always good to have someone with a rifle. The other day someone was here and he told us he'd heard there are animals which are sometimes seen in the area of the Pass. So it's good the *askari* is armed – you never know, do you?' He laughed a little and shook hands. 'Good to see you boys. Come again on your way back. Goodbye – and good luck.'

Now we were on the last lap of our journey, which would last only an hour or two. About halfway to the Pass, our calm, reticent *askari* suddenly became agitated. 'Stop!' he said. We obeyed. He opened the door of the truck and jumped out onto the road. Within three seconds he had raised his rifle to his shoulder – and fired! He ran into the bush; we followed. After about 100 yards or so, he fell on one knee. He was holding the horns of a gazelle; it had fallen to the ground, wounded by a shoulder shot. The *askari* drew a knife from its sheath. He turned the gazelle's head so that its throat was facing the *askari*. The *askari* firmly recited the Arabic ritual, '*Bis milai, raham, raheem. El hamdullilah!*' Without hesitation, the *askari* cut the throat of the gazelle; by slitting the gazelle's throat while the animal was still alive, the *askari* was adhering to Islamic law. The dead animal was then carried back to our truck.

Abdi, the cook, glanced at the gazelle, then he said, 'You are Christians; but we follow the teaching of Mohamed. Your Christmas is a great feast. When we have made our camp, I and the *askari* will skin the gazelle. There will be plenty of meat for us. I will cut out the fillet so that you have the best meat for your feast. The *askari* is a good shot. He did not shoot the gazelle through the heart; he made a shoulder shot. This way we followed the teaching of Mohamed. Never eat dead meat because it might be unclean, especially if the body of a dead animal has been lying in the hot sun. To make sure the meat is fresh, you must always kill an animal which is alive. The *askari* did a perfect job! As long as we follow the teaching of Mohamed, we will be happy and healthy. But we also have respect for your religion. Jesus was a great prophet.'

We were awestruck by the views from the Sheikh Pass. With our upbringing within the confines of England, we had not yet experienced the magnificent wonders of the wider world. For some minutes, we did not speak at all, as our senses tried to take in the majesty of the mountains which rose before our eyes from every quarter. It was not long before Abdi announced he had found a beautiful camp site, which at the same time was sheltered by huge, towering black rocks. Apparently, we had left the sand behind because the ground was stony; as we walked around we could feel underfoot that some of the stones were sharp. Little time was lost in unpacking and organising our belongings. While we sat at a camp table with a beer in front of each of us, Abdi and the *askari* carried the gazelle away to be skinned.

A few hours later – spent entranced by the beauty of an unforgettable sunset – it was almost time for dinner. In locations which are not far from the equator, the twilight is of very short duration. Once the sun had set, darkness would soon follow, and so it was that night in the stillness of the Sheikh Pass. Our camp site was enlivened by a fire whose flames made quick work of the dry pieces of wood we had collected before sundown. Apart from the crackling and sparks which flew out of the fire, our whole environment seemed to be serenely peaceful.

We chatted amiably, telling one another stories of our experiences, anecdotes of our lives, which at that time represented for each of us about 20 years on earth. We suggested to the *askari* that since he would be guarding us through the hours of sleep, he might benefit from taking a nap for a few hours. He said he would, but only after enjoying his dinner of the 'hallaled' meat of the gazelle. As for ourselves, Abdi had prepared a delicious meal which had, as its high point, the fillet of the gazelle. Our meal was enhanced by a bottle of good red wine.

In the late evening the temperature dropped quite quickly. So we withdrew from the chilly air by sliding into our sleeping bags. Each of us had a 'Hounsfield' bed; I still have mine to this day. Disassembled, the Hounsfield needed very little space; the thin steel rods could easily be placed side by side and wrapped in the canvas of the camp bed. Having easily joined the telescopic rods, each of us lay snugly in our sleeping bags, our bodies supported a few inches above the ground by the canvas of the bed.

At about 11 o'clock, John Whitmore announced that, in an hour, Christmas Day would be upon us, so why not sing some Christmas carols, which we did. The words of *O Come All Ye Faithful* or *Hark the Herald Angels Sing*, sung as tunefully as our untrained voices would permit, could be heard gently carried into the blackness which enveloped the Sheikh Pass, and I soon began to drift off to sleep. Before falling asleep, I took a last look around me. The fire was still burning brightly and around the fire were our three camp beds. Opposite mine, I could see the form of our *askari* guard; he stood there, motionless. Looking up to the heavens the night sky was brilliant with stars. Just before falling asleep I identified the Great Bear (Ursa Major) and the constellation of Orion. As I was slowly and gently losing consciousness, I heard one of my companions say, 'It's midnight – Happy Christmas.' Then I slipped into a totally relaxed slumber.

Suddenly, I was awake – or was I dreaming? I looked up to see the stars; there were no stars to be seen! Above me, there was only blackness. Then I felt stones under my back. Looking up again, I could see the outline of what seemed to be some sort of wide overhang; what was it? Then I told myself I was having a dream as I seemed to be lying under the extended tailboard of a truck; yes, this must be a dream.

Then I heard above me a deep, heaving pant. Now I was suddenly awake – and I sensed I was in danger. There was no time to try and reason any more. I have no recollection of how I extricated myself from my quite narrow, limiting sleeping bag. But now I was running away, barefoot over the stones, from the threatening danger; some of the stones were sharp enough to cut into my feet. Feeling desperately terrified I could see, straight ahead of me, the outline of a bush. Without hesitation I threw myself headlong into the centre of the dense, thorny branches. Cut and scratched, I crouched in that bush. I could feel my heart pounding. I tried to cry out, but no sound came; my throat felt utterly dry and I was breathless with fear. I crouched there, a terrified, pitiful shadow of my usual self, staring into the blackness of the night, waiting…

I did not have to wait long. As I was peering in the direction of our little camp, I saw a lion: The lion was walking slowly and deliberately towards me. Now it was about six yards (five metres) in front of me. I made no attempt to escape. I looked at the lion, mesmerised. I could not move and, looking back, I suppose I was frozen with fear.

The lion stopped; it was standing in front of me. My unblinking eyes were glued to the lion's head. The lion slowly raised and turned its head, as though its senses were testing the air for a scent. The head turned back. Was the lion looking at me just as I was staring at it? Although I could see the form of the beast, I could not see its eyes. Was the lion looking at me, or perhaps into my eyes? How was I to tell? I was still feeling terribly frightened. Just a few seconds later the lion, which was so close that in the darkness I could see quite clearly not only its form but also its long, lithe and very strong body, slowly advanced towards me – and then turned to its left. In a purposeful but somehow unhurried way, this strikingly powerful animal strode away into the blackness of the night.

Now I was feeling exhausted and sick. A strong voice rang out, cutting through the night air. 'Colin! Are you still in the land of the living?' My tremulous reply was brief and to the point. 'Yes!' I walked barefoot back to our camp. After welcoming my return to some sort of normality, one of our group said that when he woke up he had seen the 'big cat' sitting on its hind quarters by the fire.

Then the *askari* described what he had seen. Perhaps feeling tired and a little sleepy, he was brought back to reality when he found himself looking at a lion which, unexpectedly, found itself in our camp. The *askari* thought the most likely explanation was that the lion had smelled the blood of the gazelle skin and had been tempted to investigate the situation.

The *askari* explained that when he saw the lion in our camp area, he was at a loss as to what he should do in the darkness. In any case, the *askari* let out a shout, whereupon the lion decided to leave us. The lion saw his exit path as past my bed: he needed to avoid the fire. The *askari* saw the lion jump over the fire and pad away, however, as one of its legs passed by the bottom of my camp bed, it caught the protruding steel rod of the bed's frame. This turned the bed over and I was thrown onto the stony ground. When I was suddenly awoken, I was lying, unknowingly, under a part of the lion's body which totally blocked my view of the starlit heavens. Still encased in the confines of my sleeping bag, at that moment I must have been very close to the lion's chest, or possibly the head, so when I had looked up expecting to see the stars, my sight was blocked by the massive hulk of the cat.

On Christmas Day we lost little time in departing from the magnificent Sheikh Pass. After all, if we received another visitor there was no guarantee that the animal would be so understanding to us as our earlier visitor! We travelled back to Hargeisa, there to await instructions for our next posting.

A few days later, I received a short message to say I should call on the company commander at 3 p.m. Major John Roche welcomed me with a benevolent smile. 'It's so good to see you, Colin,' he said. 'You already have a reputation around here. They call you "the lion man". I gather we might have lost you.' He smiled again. Then he went on, 'I have been thinking a bit about your next posting. In fact, I have discussed the subject with the Colonel, Humphrey French. We agreed you need a pleasant change; you definitely earned it. We posted you 100 miles south of Hargeisa, to Awareh. Then you were on detachment to Gourdoumi; you saw too much bloodshed there. It's amazing what the Somalis will do to take over a watering hole for their camels; they just fight to the death! There would have been even more bloodshed if you hadn't stood your ground and kept them apart at Gourdoumi. And we had no idea at the time that the captain you reported to was an alcoholic. You certainly had a difficult time.

'Anyway, this country is threatened by a huge plague of locusts. We are told that they will eat just about *everything*. There is a team here to help the government to try to do something about it. Because of the seriousness of the situation, the government has asked your Colonel for assistance. They have asked for one of our officers to be made available: the Colonel, on my advice, has selected you for the assignment.

'But there is no hurry, Colin; the locusts have not yet arrived. So for the next few weeks I would like you to help out in Burao. Then, if the government needs your support, you should be ready for this at short notice. Now you can leave for Burao. There you can give a hand with administrative matters; also, within the next couple of weeks bring your reports and any other outstanding things up to date. Then, when you are needed, you will be ready to return to Hargeisa and report to the senior locust control adviser to the government; he is based in the secretariat in Hargeisa.

'So now proceed to Burao. Assuming your services will be needed, once you get the call, move fast! Thank you for helping out. I am sure you will be a success. Goodbye, Colin.'

Was I embarking on a more peaceful phase of my military service in Somaliland? I could only hope for the best in that foreign environment. In any case, I could only do my best. For me, that was always my simple maxim.

2

Luk Haiyah

A few weeks later, while I was helping with some administrative duties in Burao, word came that I should start my detachment with the Desert Locust Control (DLC). It was time to say goodbye to my company commander of the Somaliland Scouts. John Roche had explained that, although my services would be lent to the DLC, this would not change my status as a military officer. And I would never be alone in my work. Major Roche had issued instructions that I would be supported by a section of eight Somali soldiers, or *askaris*; the section was under the leadership of Sergeant Abdi. I found Sergeant Abdi to be a courteously respectful man who seemed quietly business-like and matter-of-fact.

Sergeant Abdi suggested that, before our departure by truck, we should briefly visit the Ordnance Supply Office. 'Here, Colin,' the captain said to me, 'I have an excellent revolver for you. Someone mentioned that you are a good shot. You never know, it's always good to have a revolver. I mean, you never know.' The captain offered me the revolver. 'I don't think I will need it, but thank you anyway,' I responded, 'I suppose it might be useful. On the other hand, it's quite an attractive weapon. Someone might murder me to lay their hands on it. I've got my little cane here; I think I will stick to the cane.' Without more ado, I set off with Sergeant Abdi and the *askaris*. I felt comfortably confident that we would soon be functioning well as a team.

Our journey to Hargeisa, the main town of Somaliland, followed the usual monotonous pattern, as we steadily progressed through the semidesert conditions. Once in Hargeisa, I made contact with the government's locust control adviser. Having handed me an information package, he told me I should continue to Sillil in the north–west, where I would meet a locust control officer called Gerald Selby-Lowndes. Gerald would put me in the picture, and would probably ask me to make a reconnaissance to search for locusts and report if the locusts were breeding. The adviser also suggested that on the way, when I would pass through Borama, I should call on the district commissioner, whose name was Michael Wilson.

The next afternoon I found myself sitting in Wilson's office. As the colonial district commissioner of the Borama/Zeila area, Wilson's job was to administratively ensure that the people of the area could lead peaceful, productive lives. And who were the people who lived in the area? In the main they were members of the Issa tribe who, at that time, numbered about a million; the tribe is distributed over large areas of north–western Somaliland, Djibouti and eastern Ethiopia. The Issa had a reputation for being fearless fighters, and from time to time they quarrelled and fought with a neighbouring tribe called the Danakil. The Danakil tribe was quite wide-spread and significant numbers inhabited the former French Somaliland (Djibouti) and a part of south–eastern Ethiopia.

Michael Wilson was a delightful man who was dedicated to his work. An avowed socialist, he used to enjoy telling me about the street of houses he owned in England. I regarded him as a compassionate, socialist administrator with a capitalist heart. In time, we became firm friends.

As I sat before him he became thoughtful. Then he suddenly turned his head and gave me a hard look. 'Thank

God you're here,' he said, 'you have probably come at the right moment. The Issa are not happy – and I can understand them. But they must obey the law.'

'I'm sorry,' I interjected, 'I am not in the picture. I'm afraid I don't know what you are talking about.'

'You mean,' Wilson said, 'you weren't briefed in Hargeisa? Well, they should have told you. I am having a problem with the Issa Elders. The locusts have already arrived. It's only a question of time before ephemeral grass and maize cultivations will be devoured, that is, unless the Desert Locust Control people can kill off the invading locusts and their progeny.

'But this is the heart of the problem. A few years ago a locust plague hit this area. The method of killing locusts was to mix a very small amount of arsenic with bran. Then the bran was spread on the ground using a huge army of labourers. The locusts ate the bran and the arsenic killed them. What went wrong was that some of the labourers were lazy; they set off with the sacks of bran and arsenic; camels carried the sacks. Then once they were out of sight, instead of spreading the bran as they had been shown, they just dumped the bran by the sack load under a tree. And then they went to sleep. The livestock ate the bran in quite large quantities and died of arsenic poisoning.

'Now we have the locusts again. And the Elders have sent me a letter to say that under no circumstances will they allow the locust bait to be spread over Issa territory. I have explained to the Elders that arsenic is no longer used in the bran. The chemical, which is benzene hexachloride, is harmless to livestock. The Elders have rejected my assurance. They have stated that if anyone tries to spread the locust bait, then the person concerned will have to be killed. Their argument is that this extreme action is necessary, if the tribe's livestock is to be preserved.

'The Elders also said that the Issa associate locusts with rain and green vegetation, which is good grazing for their livestock.

21

They are afraid that if we kill the locust nymphs (which are called hoppers) and the adult locusts, then the fresh vegetation will die.'

'So what do you want me to do?' I asked.

Wilson meditated again, this time for about 30 seconds. 'I think we should go about our work – and hope for the best. I would like you to travel tomorrow to a place called Sillil, which is not far from the coastal town of Zeila. Close to Sillil, you will find the camp of the locust control officer; his name is Gerald Selby-Lowndes. You will work with him and I am sure he will appreciate your assistance. He has a large area to look after and the locust plague is intensifying. The two of you will go about your work. If there are problems, then Selby-Lowndes will be in contact with us by radio. If the voice mode is not functioning, then a message can be sent by Morse code. From now on I want you to call me "Michael"; if I may I would like to call you "Colin". Michael got up, looked me in the eye, held out his hand and said, 'Godspeed, Colin.'

In later years I would become better acquainted with Borama. Even during my initial short visit, in the context of Somaliland as a whole, it was a beautiful place which instantly fitted the phrase 'love at first sight.' Situated at an altitude of almost 5,000 feet (about 1,500 metres) above sea level, the air was fresh. And in contrast to the arid, semidesert – even desert – conditions of much of the Somali peninsula, there was an abundance of healthy-looking vegetation, including cultivated fields. In short, to spend time in Borama was a delight.

Early next morning Sergeant Abdi with myself and the *askaris* were en route to Sillil. Although the journey was only about 200 miles, we were on the road for about ten hours. The truck road to Zeila (and onwards to Djibouti) was stony and sometimes potholed, so as passengers we were subjected to vibrations and frequent braking. The aim was to average a speed of 25 mph. We rarely reached this target, and as we descended towards the coast, the lovely vegetation gradually gave way to scrub, which itself dwindled to sand as we neared Sillil. We were approaching the coastline of the Gulf of Aden, itself an extension of the Red Sea. Now our environment was humid and very hot. During the journey, although much of one's concentration and energy were inevitably consumed by how best to maintain physical resilience as our truck bounced and braked on the road's uneven surface, from time to time we passed Issa tribesmen who were walking either on the road or in the bush close-by. One was struck by the usually fine physique of these handsome people; their bodies were well built and often looked powerful, devoid of fat. Without exception, each carried a long spear.

The village of Sillil was typical of villages in Somaliland. There was only one permanent type of building: a concrete disused police station with two rooms; the windows had no glass, only four vertical iron bars. The Somali dwellings are called *gurghis*. The dwelling consists of hooped rods, the ends implanted in the ground. Heavy mats are then thrown over the hooped rods to provide protection against the elements, especially heat and blowing sand. Although a *gurghi* can serve as semi-permanent shelter, it can be quickly dismantled, so if, for example, heavy rain had fallen some distance away, then the *gurghi* could easily be dismantled, and the rods, with the matting, loaded onto a burden camel. The villagers, now forming a caravan of loaded camels, would trek to the new area of abundant grazing. There, the *gurghis* could soon be re-erected, while the camels would enjoy the fresh grazing.

For many Somalis, the better part of their lives sees their attention focused on looking after their camels and increasing the size of the herd. A camel-owner told me once that the size of the herd reflects wealth. He had started with 20 camels; now he had 80. He explained that, under his religion, he was permitted to have four wives. But for a young man with few camels, it would be irresponsible to take on more than one wife; the young man would not be rich enough to support more than one. As a rule of thumb, one should think in terms of one wife per 20 camels. It was only because he owned 80 camels, that he had reached the limit of four wives.

Having reached Sillil, Sergeant Abdi found a so-called coffee shop. Coffee shops are found in every village of Somaliland. They normally serve hot, sweet tea. Sometimes they also offer a type of bread and perhaps boiled mutton. The coffee shop owner directed us to the nearby locust control encampment. At last we had arrived. Selby-Lowndes's cook came out of a hut which had been constructed of dry branches. 'Welcome to Sillil, sir,' he said with a smile, 'Mr Gerald had to go to Zeila. He will come soon. We are expecting you. It's too hot here. Come inside and I will bring tea.'

Gerald Selby-Lowndes appeared after about a half hour. As he got out of the jeep, I noticed he was wearing only a short pair of khaki drill shorts; he was a thin man of 40 or so and he was quite tall. From head to toe his skin was a deep brown. I came to know Gerald a little. He was a delightfully unaffected, direct and friendly person and I could never have imagined he might have been discourteous or bad-tempered in any way. He always seemed calm and relaxed. Going about his work in the north–western part of Somaliland, Gerald could never have had an inkling of his impending fate.

About a year later his jeep would be washed away in a sudden flood of what was usually a dry river bed. He managed to get out of the jeep and he did his best to reach the edge of the fast-flowing torrent. There his team grabbed his hands and wrists. Although they did their utmost to pull Gerald out of the raging torrent, their Herculean efforts were in vain. Gerald drowned in their hands.

'Sorry, I wasn't here when you came, Colin. I certainly intended to be. The problem was I got stuck in a flooded area between here and Zeila. Apparently it's quite uncharacteristic for this area. I mean there has been torrential rain for about two weeks now. You get these huge downpours for one or two hours; then it's back to the heat and humidity.

You probably don't know much yet about locusts. But after all this rain, the ground is ideal for locusts to breed. In fact, two weeks ago, that's exactly what happened. A huge swarm arrived from Saudi Arabia. I tried to measure it by traversing with the jeep. I reckon it covered about 100 square miles. The adults were yellow, which means they were mature, and they were copulating over the whole coastal area. The ground was soft, so the females could easily lay their egg pods; there are 50 to 150 eggs in each pod. So the degree of multiplication is enormous. The adults have flown away to the west, over the Ethiopian border. They fly at 12 miles per hour in still air. But depending on the altitude at which the swarm is flying, they may have a tail wind. So they might cover 20 or 30 miles per hour. Yes, they are very mobile. And remember, in order to maintain itself the locust must eat at least half its own weight in food *every day*. One can't know for sure, but, depending on its density, that swarm might weigh about 35,000 tons. Imagine! It's also quite interesting to know that to survive, the adults' progeny (the hoppers) need to eat their whole weight every day.

Now we have two problems on our hands. The first is that the swarm has been breeding; so now the eggs are already beginning to hatch. The little locusts, which are nymphs, are hatching and they will soon start hopping around to look for some edible vegetation. We call the nymphs "hoppers". Before they fly away as pink, immature locusts, they will pass at about weekly intervals through five stages, or instars; each time they pass into the next instar they shed their skins. By the fourth or fifth instar, wing buds and wings develop and the hoppers start forming bands of increasing size; eventually whole armies are marching across the terrain, devouring everything along the way. As I said, in the fifth instar the hoppers develop wings. Then one day, as though their leader had blown a horn, the young locusts form a swarm – and they fly on their devouring, utterly destructive way.

Now I come to the second problem. The way we try and control locusts is to reduce the size of the next generation as much as possible. If we do a good job the "escape", as we call it, is pretty thin. Then predator birds and natural causes do the rest. The way we reduce the hopper population is by spreading poisoned bran ahead of the marching hoppers. The hoppers eat the bran – then they die of stomach poisoning. So far, so good? In this case, unfortunately not.

A couple of days ago I made a reconnaissance to Luk Haiyah, which is a village down the coast eastwards from here. As usual, the locals were pleasant enough, but when I asked them about locusts their whole attitude changed. Yes, swarms had crossed the coast and they had seen some breeding. They said they would show me some egg fields. Then they said I should go away. They said the locusts bring rain, which is good for the grazing of their livestock. I explained to them that in a way they were right. The monsoon wind does bring rain; but the wind also carries the locusts. It's the monsoon that produces rain, not the locusts which arrive at the same time. I also told them that unless the hoppers are controlled, that is destroyed, then the next locust generation will eat up the ephemeral grazing.

While we were talking, a group of Elders joined us. The senior Elder said that he had been listening to us. He wanted to make something very clear to me. A year or two ago there had been an invasion of locusts. In those days arsenic was used as the poison ingredient of the bran. Some livestock had eaten the bran, which made the animals very ill: in fact, some had died. There was to be no repetition! The Elders were there to advise their people. They had already issued their advice, which was that if any intruder into their territory was found to be laying locust bait, then the person involved must be killed at once.

I tried to start a discussion on the subject, but the Elders remained stubbornly disinterested in talking further. They advised me to leave as soon as possible which, they added, would be in my own interest. They did lend me a man for a couple of hours, who showed me some very large locust egg fields. He had a really expert eye. When he spotted an egg field he jumped out of the jeep and dug in the sand; then he pushed a hand into the little hole he made and grabbed a handful of sand. He let the sand filter through his fingers, which left a few egg pods on the palm of his hand. Then, with a sort of look of triumph, he turned to me and said: "*Eiyaha!*" – which in Somali means locusts. From what I could see, the egg fields were very extensive.

So now we have a problem, Colin. On the one hand, we are here to control locusts; on the other, we are working amongst people who will kill us if we go about our work. It's not exactly a pleasant scenario, I must say.

The reason I went to Zeila this morning was to send a telegram to the district commissioner, Michael Wilson. I had tried my radio transmitter, but I couldn't make contact; maybe the heat and humidity caused interference – who knows? In any case, Wilson represents the government of the Protectorate, so it's his responsibility to decide what is to be done. I expect a reply tomorrow, so I will visit Zeila again to pick it up. If you would like, we can go together.'

At six o'clock the following morning I found myself sitting next to Gerald in his jeep. Behind us sat a retired sergeant-major and Sergeant Abdi who, I noticed, made a point of staying close to me virtually the whole time. The distance to Zeila was 28 miles. As we neared the town we found ourselves driving through vast flooded areas. Our driver did his best to navigate his way through what seemed like a shallow, swampy lake. Whenever possible he stuck to the relatively hard surface of the road; even so, on three occasions we were halted by wet, soft sand and the jeep, wheels spinning, gradually came to a halt. Each time, the wheels had to be freed and the vehicle jacked up so that hard boards could be placed under the wheels. At last, at ten o'clock, we arrived in Zeila. We were streaming with sweat.

In spite of the heat and humidity, my impression of Zeila was positive. The town struck me as more Arab than Somali. The solidly built block-like houses all had spotless white walls and the narrow streets were picturesque, while also ensuring the maximum possible shade and protection from the scorching sun. This was a coastal town which had served as a port and important trading centre for at least 2,000 years. Like many coastal towns the world over, Zeila's fortunes had experienced ups and downs. For long periods it had served as the main town of an area which had been colonised. Over the centuries, the colonisers had included Arab Sultans, the Ottoman Empire, Egypt and, at the end of the nineteenth century, the British. In addition to trading activities along the coast and with Yemen, the town had strong trading links with Harar and the Ogaden Province of Ethiopia.

Gerald's first port of call was an Arab merchant, to whom I was introduced. Mr Mahmud, dressed in a long white robe, was a charming man in his 40s. His office, on the first floor of a large house, was spacious and airy; near the window a servant sat and constantly pulled on a thin rope which activated a huge fan. Mr Mahmud welcomed me to Zeila; he hoped we might see one another from time to time. At this moment Gerald produced a cheque book and handed Mr Mahmud the cheque. Then Mr Mahmud turned to me. 'I am a bit like a bank for the British,' he said. Then he went on, 'This cheque is for quite a big amount. I suppose Gerald has to pay the workers. It doesn't matter. So long as it is the British, I can give you any amount. The British never fail you. I have never been let down by the British; you can always trust them. If ever I can help you, in any way, please do not hesitate to visit me. Goodbye Lieutenant Everard.'

Our next stop was the post office. Gerald picked up the telegram from Michael Wilson. He read it slowly. Then he spoke. 'Right, Colin,' he said, 'Now we know where we stand. The district commissioner states it is the policy of the government to control the locust invasion. This policy will be applied. Wilson will arrive in Sillil the day after tomorrow. He wants to be briefed by me. I will then return to Hargeisa. My supervisor, who is an experienced locust control man, will advise the DC. Wilson writes here that the day after his arrival in Sillil he will travel to Luk Haiyah. I have to organise a couple of trucks which will carry loads of the poisoned locust bait. He says you and your men will travel with him and that on his arrival in Sillil, he will explain your role to you. I find this message clear enough. Now we can get back to Sillil.'

Two days later, in the afternoon, Gerald had finished briefing Michael Wilson. This very nice man, Gerald Selby-Lowndes, shook my hand and said goodbye. He hoped we would meet again, but this was not to be. All one could do was to cherish the memory of a very good person.

The following morning, before our departure for Luk Haiyah, a message was delivered asking me to meet with Wilson immediately. He explained he would shortly be leaving for Luk Haiyah. There he would try to meet the Elders so that the problem of their refusal to accept the spreading of locust bait might be resolved. He wanted to avoid a confrontation, if possible. In any case, something that could not be avoided was the application of the government's policy. With this in mind, he intended to demonstrate the will of the government by organising a symbolic action by spreading locust bait; if he was unable to find local labour to do this, he would do it himself, assisted by the staff who accompanied him. As far as I was concerned, he emphasised that he wanted the military to maintain a low profile. He would ask for me to intervene only as a very last resort.

And this would be if the whole operation became unmanageable for him.

With a clear understanding of our roles, we left in convoy for Luk Haiyah. The first vehicle carried the DC, Michael Wilson. Then came three trucks; two were loaded with sacks of locust bait, while the other carried water, food and tentage. I brought up the rear in a jeep-type vehicle; behind me a military truck transported the eight *askaris*. With the heat of the sun making itself felt, we slowly followed the sandy track to Luk Haiyah. For most of the time the route ran by the sea. Sometimes we were close to the water and one could see the dorsal fins of young sharks speeding through the shallow waves. By late afternoon we had all arrived. The locust control supervisor signalled that we should head for a low, rounded ridge where the terrain slightly rose, to survey our surroundings. Within the hour, the camp was well established. Bearing in mind Wilson's instructions, I ensured that our military detachment was positioned a short distance from the camp of the DC. During the evening there was no contact between the DC's group and my detachment.

I believe none of us slept well that night. My sleep was punctuated by the blowing of horns and long, loud, deep-throated shouts. I got up at dawn and looked around from the elevated ridge in the semidesert. I could see hundreds of men on all sides, some huddled together in small groups. Their excited voices were strong and loud. It was as though we were loosely surrounded by a jostling, noisy crowd, many of whom were young, fighting men.

Sergeant Abdi joined me and explained that the Issa had spent the night assembling their people: the horns and shouting had relayed their message; that the tribe was under threat and all who heard the appeal for help should assemble, ready to fight for their tribe, at Luk Haiyah. Practically all the men were armed with spears; some wore heavy leather belts with long knives. Sergeant Abdi pointed out a few men who were carrying thick leather shields. Others carried slings of thin, intertwined rope. Sergeant Abdi told me that the Issa were expert in the use of slings. Having loaded a stone, the user would rotate the sling at high speed above his head. Once a good speed had been generated the stone would be released, travelling at high speed to its target. He said some of the Issa achieved uncanny accuracy with their slings.

A little later I visited Michael Wilson in his tent. He looked dismayed and tired. He told me his invitation to the Elders to meet him for discussions had been rejected. With a weary look of resignation, he said that in one hour, the symbolic laying of locust bait would take place. This could be done not far from our camp, and the bait could be spread directly from the back of the trucks.

I returned to my section and explained the situation to Sergeant Abdi and the *askaris*. Then I instructed the section to make ready their rifles for action at a moment's notice. Each *askari* should personally ensure he had an ample reserve of ammunition. Now we were prepared.

An hour later, the trucks loaded with locust bait were led away from our elevated encampment by Wilson, who was on foot. I shadowed the operation in an open truck; I sat with the driver while Sergeant Abdi and the *askaris* stood in the truck behind us.

We hardly had to wait five minutes for a reaction. I had been briefly distracted; glancing towards the coast, I was struck by the beautiful sight of sand dunes and the calm, blue sea beyond. All of a sudden my idyllic view was violently interrupted. A wave of frenzied humanity rose up before our eyes, charging straight towards us. About 200 men were bearing down on us with great purpose; the very loud, angry shouting was punctuated by high-pitched, venomous shrieks. The glistening spears and the blades of long knives caught the rays of the strong sun and I, for one, was almost mesmerised by the flashing of steel above the heads of the shouting attackers.

Michael Wilson strode towards the tribesmen and held up his hand. Now the throng was about 60 yards in front of him. Wilson spoke to them in Somali. The horde stopped and their members sank to the ground; they seemed to be listening. With hindsight, I doubted that Wilson's broken, poorly pronounced Somali was comprehensible, except possibly to a few. I quietly, but firmly, instructed Sergeant Abdi and the *askaris to* load their rifles and to kneel in the firing position. Sergeant Abdi said that, as far as he could understand, Wilson was appealing to the tribesmen to retreat and he would later talk with them. Then a high-pitched, strong voice rang out. Sergeant Abdi translated again: 'The bullets are like the wind; they will never hurt us. Kill them!' A moment later the wave, which now seemed more like a wall of humanity, rose up as one.

And the shouting tribesmen charged.

I walked in front of the firing line and took hold of Wilson's arm. The man was trembling and looked distraught. 'Lieutenant Everard,' he said in a low, tremulous voice, 'I have failed. Please restore order.' Now the shouting, crazed tribesmen were close upon us.

'Michael,' I replied, 'I cannot restore order as long as you are standing right in front of the firing line.' I quickly led Wilson back; he was sobbing. Then I heard thuds. The Issa were bringing their slings into action.

At that moment my thoughts ran to a scene I had witnessed near Gourdoumi a few months earlier. After a tribal battle over water and grazing, the bodies of those killed had been loaded into a covered truck. I had looked at those bodies and, without exception, the testicles of the dead men had been severed and pressed into the mouths of the owners. Was a similar fate about to overtake me? Our attackers were close to us; in a few seconds they would overpower and kill us.

For my personal defence I was holding a short cane. The captain who had offered me a revolver had been right when he had said that you never know!

'FIRE!' I ordered. 'FIRE!' After the second salvo, the organised charge stopped – and disintegrated before us. Most of the attackers fell to the ground and crawled away. There was one pocket of resistance which defiantly stood there, glaring at us. I took a rifle from one of the *askaris*. I strode towards the men, motioning that they should retreat. When I was about ten yards from them, one raised his spear horizontally at the shoulder. Who would strike first? I raised the rifle and had his legs in the sights. He turned and fled; the others followed him.

Once the area was clear of tribesmen, we picked up the wounded and they were sent to the hospital in Zeila for treatment. To my astonishment, but not to the surprise of Sergeant Abdi, only three attackers had been shot and wounded. With a suggestion of a knowing smile, Sergeant Abdi explained that in similar circumstances, experience had shown that it was too much to expect Somali soldiers to kill their own brother Somalis. The last thing a soldier wanted to live with was the blood of a fellow Somali on his hands. The way out for the soldiers was to shoot a little above the heads of the attackers. As far as I was concerned, this was a good thing; I was relieved that our task had been completed with relatively little bloodshed.

On my return to Zeila I received a message that the military detachment would end and I should return to Hargeisa for re-assignment. The DLC had recruited more staff and two would shortly arrive in Sillil to deal with the infestation of hoppers. They would have armed police protection.

After my return to England later that year, I was demobilised. With the encouragement of my father, I embarked on a commercial career. Although my efforts met with success,

Figure 1. Philip Stephenson C.M.G., the director of the Desert Locust Survey and the Desert Locust Control. Under Stephenson's able direction (1949–61) remarkable research and technological progress was achieved in controlling the desert locust scourge.

after two years I concluded that pure commerce was not for me. I preferred to be involved in an activity which had more 'soul'. I had enjoyed the locust experience and the activity struck me as worthwhile, in the sense that if one's efforts to control a locust infestation were successful, then without question starvation of the population would be prevented. In other words, if grazing and crops could be saved from the locust scourge, then famine could be avoided.

So in 1952 I wrote to Philip Stephenson, who was the director of the DLC; he immediately arranged for me to be recruited as a locust control field officer. My recruitment was organised by the Crown Agents in London.

During my interview, it was explained that I would become a member of the largest (from a financial aspect) department within the East Africa High Commission (EAHC). The establishment in 1948 of the Commission was a far-sighted initiative of the British Government. The Commission had no direct connection with the British Colonial Administrative Service, rather, its main objective was to stimulate economic development (for example, through the use of a common East African currency) and to provide services of a common nature to the participating governments of Kenya, the then Tanganyika, and Uganda.

By way of further explanation, apart from overseeing and co-ordinating with institutions and enterprises such as the East African Judiciary, or the East African Railways and Harbours Corporation, the Commission directly operated about 20 departments ranging from East African income tax to some ten scientific research departments in the fields of medicine, agriculture, forestry and fisheries. These departments were established in various locations within the three participating countries.

The only department which operated internationally – that was, beyond the East African borders in a physical sense – was the DLC. Given the economic importance of agriculture in East Africa, efficient operation of the DLC was regarded as of primary importance in terms of protecting agriculture.

The DLC maintained a strong connection with the Anti-Locust Research Centre in London and dove-tailed its operations with the national locust control organisations in some ten countries to the north of East Africa, extending to the Persian Gulf.

The East Africa High Commission was succeeded in 1965 by the East African Common Services Organization

Figure 2. North–western Somaliland, 1953. Issa tribesmen.

(EACSO). A few years later, EACSO was replaced by the East African Community (EAC). The Administrator of EACSO was A.L. Adu (from Ghana) and the Administrator of the EAC was Dunstan Omari, from Tanzania; I was privileged to have regular consultative contact with both of these excellent men.

At the end of 1952, shortly before my 22nd birthday, I flew to Hargeisa. For my first field assignment I was sent to Sillil. The armed police who had been designated to assure my safety knew of my former military role. They told me that the Elders who had attempted to disrupt and stop the locust control field operations, had been tried and convicted of incitement to violence, attempted murder and of causing a serious disturbance of the peace. Understandably, I approached Sillil with apprehension.

Now that I was again in Sillil, the constables were concerned about my safety. They could not rule out revenge. On my arrival, the constables requested me to sleep in the disused former police station, instead of sleeping in a tent. In the depth of the first night, at about 2 a.m., I was awoken. In the moonlight I could see the face of a constable. He was holding the bars of the glassless window. 'Mr Everard,' he said, 'Would you please move into the other room? With such a bright moon an attacker can throw a spear between the bars and the spear will strike your head or throat. Thank you, sir.'

A few days later the local Elders presented me with a young goat. They wanted to talk to me. The senior of the Elders spoke first, 'Mr Everard, two of us were recently released from prison. We remember you well as a military man. You had your duty to do. Now you are a civilian. We and our people respect the work you are doing to save our grazing and crops. We want you to know we hold no grudge against you and we have told our tribe that at all times you must be permitted to do your work, without any interference. This evening we will perform our very special dances for you. We hope you will enjoy the dancing. Thank you for helping us.' Yes, the Issa are very special.

It was a great party.

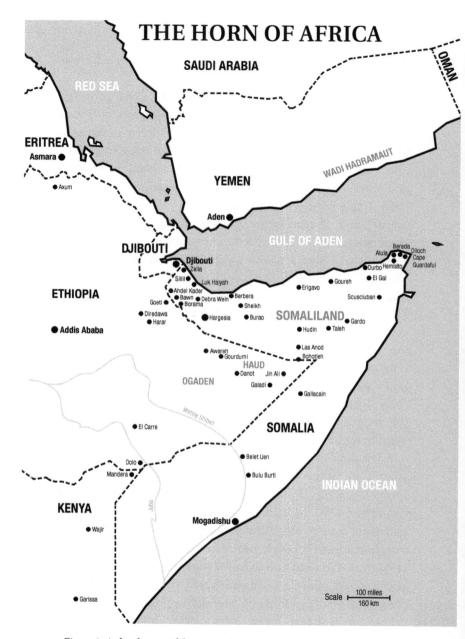

Figure 3. A sketch map of the 1950s, showing the Somali-populated area of the
Horn of Africa, an area which, through the ages, has been severely ravaged
by desert locust plagues. Places detailed in the text are shown on the map.

3

The Locust Life

After completing the Sillil assignment, I was asked to transfer to a base near Borama. A town in the hills, Borama is situated about 80 miles north–west of Somaliland's main town, Hargeisa. I had visited Borama a year or two earlier during the period of my military service. I soon found a camp site and, after calling on the main administrative offices in Borama, took stock of the situation.

In general terms, the area I should keep under surveillance for locust activity was not large; the total ground might correspond to a rectangle of about 200 by 100 miles. However, I soon realised there was only one truck road. This ran roughly north–south through the area; its surface was dirt which from time to time became potholed. Apart from this road, there were a number of camel tracks; some of these might be traversable with a four-wheel drive jeep-type vehicle. But taking into account that much of the terrain was hilly and stony, if a camel track was to be used for vehicles, then the track would first need to be tested for its practicality.

As a first step, I would study a map produced by the British Ordnance Survey in order to select key areas where camel tracks might be used by vehicles; apart from the possibilities presented by camel tracks, in certain low-lying areas one could use *wadis* to penetrate the area with vehicles. In Somali these *wadis* were.called *tougs*. A *toug* could be used as a sort of road, although one needed to be careful of two possibilities. First, after rain in the hills the normally dry *toug* would be converted into a fast-flowing river, sometimes for several hours. So when driving along a *toug* one needed to pay constant attention to means of escape, if one were to be confronted with a wave of water, which sometimes might be several feet high. Second, was the importance of avoiding the wells which had been dug by the tribesmen. Apart from the risk of causing water contamination, if a jeep's wheel should inadvertently find itself sinking on the edge of the wall of a well, the effort and time needed to recover the vehicle could be seemingly endless.

As a desert locust control field officer, what did I need to know and what key challenges would confront me?

Although the Anti-Locust Research Centre (ALRC) in London developed a generic locust reporting system which covered some 60 countries, in fact the desert locust (*Schistocerca gregaria*) most often *directly* affects some 21 Frontline countries (see explanation below and the list in the Appendix) in the western, north and north–eastern countries of Africa, the Arabian peninsula as well as some western countries of Asia, for example India and Pakistan.

As an aside, nowadays the Food and Agriculture Organization (a specialised agency of the United Nations) uses a forecasting and reporting system which is more refined than the system which had been developed by the ALRC. In the context of desert locusts, FAO (through its desert locust technical group) classifies 21 countries as 'Frontline' countries. FAO also lists a further 29 countries as 'Invasion' countries. Invasion countries are those which do not normally support locust populations, but, given certain ecological conditions, they may well be invaded by desert locust swarms; and these swarms may breed, resulting in

Figure 4. The ravenous desert locust – Schistocerca gregaria. *Since biblical times, the desert locust has ravaged crops and grazing in some 50 countries.*

infestations of ravenous locust nymphs, or hoppers. So in what might be called the 'big picture', there are altogether 50 countries which are vulnerable to locust plagues.

Other locust species include the African Migratory locust and the Red locust. When locusts are in the gregarious phase, they stay together in swarms, some of which are huge. For example, the size of one swarm was compared to the size of Greater London. As an order of magnitude, in the Somali peninsula, which is often called the Horn of Africa, we anticipated two desert locust invasions a year; these invasions were carried on the monsoon winds. Each invasion equated to about 1,000 square miles of locust swarms.

Part of the work of the locust field officer was to carry out regular, systematic reconnaissance of the area under his responsibility. If locust activity was observed, then a report was sent, giving details. In this way, over the years, the migratory routes of locusts could be forecast.

In the 1920s, Sir Boris Uvarov, a brilliant Russian scientist who settled in England, made ground-breaking discoveries relating to locust behaviour. His book, *Grasshoppers and Locusts*, shed critical light on previously unknown knowledge of locust behaviour, including his Phase theory, that under certain environmental conditions, solitary locusts breed and their offspring behave in a gregarious manner. These gregarious locusts form swarms which, in turn, cause devastating damage to crops and grassland. In a number of countries, the ravaging locust eats entire crops and, in consequence people may starve to death. Some of these starving people hang themselves on trees, a quick death being the preferred option.

The adult female desert locust weighs about three grams, the male, a little less than two grams, and they measure 3 inches in length (7.5 centimetres). In still air, a locust flies at 12 miles per hour. With a monsoon wind of, say, 40 mph, a locust swarm may travel 200 miles or more in one day, devouring crops and grazing along the way. Because the monsoon winds bring precipitation, the female locusts find soft sand or loam into which they can lay their egg pods. Typically, a female lays three times, usually at intervals of several days. On average, each egg pod contains about 80 eggs. It goes without saying, therefore, that the generation multiplication rate is colossal.

Once the female has completed her egg-laying cycle, she dies. Depending on the temperature and humidity in the sand or soft loam, the eggs which have been deposited in pods may remain underground for one or two weeks, sometimes longer. Egg fields become visible to the practised eye; also, local locust scouts are employed to search for egg fields and report on their extent. The locust scouts may dig up some pods to gauge when the eggs might hatch. When the eggs hatch, the nymphs, which are commonly called 'hoppers', force their way to the surface and collect into hopping bands. This stage is called the 'first instar'. The hoppers shed their skins after

Figure 5. South–eastern Ethiopia, 1953. A small part of a swarm of desert locusts. Typically, the Horn of Africa suffered two invasions of locust swarms each year. Each invasion equated roughly to 1,000 square miles (2,600 square kilometres).

about a week, and the hoppers then progress into the 'second instar'. There are five instars in all, with the hoppers shedding their skins to progress. Once the third instar is reached, the hoppers organise themselves into large bands and they march in swathes across the terrain, eating the vegetation as they march. In the fourth instar the hopper develops wing buds; these become fully developed when the fifth instar is completed, and such hoppers eat their own weight in food daily. Finally they become a fully developed adult locust, which is pink in colour.

Left in their natural state, the young locust adults become increasingly active as the days pass. The locusts are already ravenous and fly at a low level in thick, concentrated clusters, looking to devour every form of vegetation. Then, after a week or ten days, the locusts suddenly form a swarm, perhaps several square miles in extent. As though a horn has been sounded, at a given moment the millions of locusts rise at once into the air. Now the swarm is on the move, usually carried by a strong monsoon wind. In order to survive, the adult locust needs to eat at least half of its own weight in food every day. Especially when the swarm comes to roost at twilight, every possible form of vegetation is devoured. Typically, one swarm will eat 30–40,000 tons of food every day.

Obviously, the size and density of swarms vary. However, as an order of magnitude, an average swarm density equates to about 15 million locusts per square mile. So when one takes into account the huge multiplication in numbers resulting from breeding, then the number of locusts on the move becomes astronomical.

The swarms which invaded the Horn of Africa usually started their flight in the Arabian peninsula. During their traverse of the Horn area, provided the twice-yearly rains had softened the sandy soil, the mature locusts would breed, depositing the egg pods in the sand. As the young, pink locusts matured, their colour would change to a solid yellow, indicating that they were ready to breed.

Anyone who has watched and heard a massive, dense swarm in flight will retain a life-long memory. As one looks up to the heavens, one sees countless locusts passing overhead, the silvery colour of their wings caught in the rays of the sun. As one's ears pick up the low hum of the millions of flying insects, one stands there as though mesmerised. Above all, one develops a feeling of utter helplessness. And for the locust control officer, such as myself, a simple thought surfaces: *What am I supposed to do?*

In fact, a great deal could be done. Through the reporting of the movements of locust swarms, a good deal had been learned about locust migratory routes, the anticipated timing of invasions and likely breeding areas. This was why, in the spring of 1953, I found myself camped near

Borama. My job was to keep the area under surveillance for locust movements.

The strategy of controlling locusts in eastern Africa had as its main aim the detection of locust egg fields in the Horn of Africa; the application of this strategy extended westwards through Ethiopia and southwards to northern Kenya. Provided sufficient information could be gathered on the movements and breeding of locusts, then a campaign could be planned and launched to destroy the locust nymphs (the hoppers) before they matured into young, flying locusts. So, once a locust campaign began, some six or seven weeks would elapse before the so-called escape of the surviving locusts would take place. If the campaign was successful, the escape would be relatively small and many of the surviving locusts would be eaten by predators, mainly birds; others would die through the effect of adverse weather conditions.

To this end, locust control officers were given responsibility for the surveillance and control of locusts within a given geographical area. Provided the locust campaigns were successful, not only would grazing for nomadic Somalis be preserved, but also significant crops throughout Ethiopia, southern Somalia, Kenya, Uganda and Tanzania would be saved from destruction.

If for some reason the new generation of locusts escaped from the northern areas on a large scale, then crops throughout eastern Africa could be destroyed. Many in East Africa recalled devastating invasions of locusts in the 1930s and 1940s. They related how dense locust swarms totally blocked the light of the sun. The railway system became paralysed due to spinning locomotive wheels, as squelching locusts nullified the contact between the wheels and the rail.

In the 1950s, the control of locusts hoppers relied entirely on ground operations. The method used required a mixture of bran and poison to be spread in the path of the marching bands of hoppers. The ravenous hoppers were attracted to the bran, ate it – and died of stomach poisoning. It was of obvious importance that the bait used would kill only the hoppers, and not other wild animals or livestock. So the mixture was about 99 per cent bran and a maximum of 1 per cent poison. The main chemical used was Agrocide also known as Lindane, which was developed and manufactured by Imperial Chemical Industries. Another chemical used was Dieldrin, produced by the Shell Company.

Some ten years later, the detection and destruction of locust swarms had evolved such that it was mainly carried out by reconnaissance and spraying aircraft. This method was employed only after much complex, meticulous experimentation had been undertaken. Certainly in 1953, the possibility of using aircraft to control locusts played no part in our planning approach.

To resume, as for my camp near Borama, it was basic. I slept in a tent; the furniture comprised a wooden camp table and a canvas chair. In a corner rested a Tilley kerosene pressure lamp. A few yards away, the cook had made a square of stones, with which he cooked simple food over a fire. Around the camp was a *zariba* (a protective barrier) of *acacia* thorn branches; the small gap for entry was closed at night. A watchman was employed to keep an eye on the camp, especially when I was away with my helpers. His remuneration was quite low; however, in addition to his pay he received a daily all-important ration of rice and dates.

The work routine of the locust control officer was essentially flexible. The concept of working hours never arose; this was a 24 hours a day job and no one would ever question this reality. One of the few fixed events of the day was the wireless network at 7 a.m. Conducted by the senior field officer, up-to-date reports were exchanged relating to every type of locust activity. So the element of co-ordination and togetherness was strongly present on a daily basis.

The successful locust field officer displayed characteristics of intelligent planning based on knowledge, the flexibility

Figure 6. Northern Somalia, 1957. L to R, Senior Research Officer Clifford Ashall with Field Officer John Funnell and Colin Everard, taking a rest after a hard day's desert locust reconnaissance.

to react quickly and with common sense in the face of changing locust movements, resourcefulness, resilience in the face of disappointment and, perhaps above all, relentless and persevering hard work.

It was in March 1953 that we learned from the daily wireless network that locust swarms had been seen crossing the coast of Somaliland, having flown over the Red Sea and the Gulf of Aden. This was the beginning of an invasion of swarms that would cover about 1,000 square miles.

It was always possible, even probable, that the area around Borama would be invaded by locust swarms. In anticipation of this, I had prioritised how one might reach certain areas where the terrain seemed suitable for the locusts to breed.

The ability to reach breeding areas fast was certainly desirable, not only to monitor egg fields, but subsequently to bring in many tons of locust bait which would need to be spread by labourers ahead of the marching hoppers. One could, of course, hire camels to transport the bait to a given area; however, this is a slow method compared to the use of motorised transport. On average, camels walk at about two and a half miles per hour, whereas a truck will travel significantly faster, even in rough terrain.

Since establishing my camp, I had compiled a sketch map of possible routes which could be used by motorised transport. In the light of the locust invasion which was already underway in coastal areas, I sat with the supervisor, a driver and some local Issa workers and showed them my sketch. After a short discussion, we agreed that the routes I had drawn made sense, with one exception. The area north-east of Borama lacked a route for accessibility. Did anyone present have ideas? Yes, one of the Issa helpers said he knew of a camel track which led into the area; the area was called the *Debra Wein*. The English translation for this was 'Large *sanseveria*'. The Issa explained that the *sanseveria* plants grew only over a part of the general area; once you descended into a sort of valley, there were no *sanseveria* plants. Nevertheless, the whole area was called the Debra Wein. He told me that he had walked in the area and there were many Kudu antelope there; their main food – the *sanseveria* – was found on the higher, flat terrain. I then consulted the Ordnance Survey map and tried to pinpoint the area. With some difficulty I found where one should expect to see 'Debra Wein'. Instead, I found a white patch; then I read the small, but clear, black print: 'Unsurveyed'.

Two days later, with a slightly quickening heart, I was en route in a Land Rover. Along with the driver, I took the supervisor and the Issa helper. We took food and water for two days. The objective was to test the feasibility of using motor transport, utilising the camel track through the Debra Wein area. My intention was that after driving in a north-easterly direction through the Debra Wein, we would turn west and eventually find the only main north–south road. We hoped to find the main road near a village called Bawn. Once on the road, we would return to our camp. The plan seemed practical and simple. I gauged the distance of the trip to be about 70 miles.

We soon found the camel track and, to my happy surprise, we found ourselves driving steadily for a few hours at about 10 mph. The track ran through partly sandy, broken country, although it was often strewn with stones and small rocks. The vegetation was scrub interspersed with *acacia* trees, their dense, bright green leaves casting a welcome shade for small groups of sheep and goats. The sun was shining from the azure above us as we progressed steadily down a long incline.

Suddenly there was a change in the landscape. Now we were beginning to traverse an extensive hill. The camel track seemed to be less well used: soon it would peter out entirely. The driving was slow as we descended to the base of the hill. We found ourselves in a wide gorge, which narrowed after only a couple of miles. Looking ahead, we could see steep walls of rock and stones rising on either side of the gorge, and my eyes came to rest on huge boulders: I estimated the walls of the gorge to have a height of between 500 and 700 feet.

I felt happy we had reached what appeared to be the entrance to the Debra Wein. Although the journey was tricky towards the end, I noted in my report that, provided work to widen and strengthen the last descending section of the track could be undertaken, it should be feasible for the track to be used by motorised transport. But of course, what lay ahead was an unknown.

Having reached the floor of the Debra Wein, we decided to make a small camp there, knowing that the sun would set by about 6 p.m. The Issa helper and the supervisor collected some camel thorn branches and encircled us with a *zariba*. The helper told us that the Debra Wein was well known as a haven for animals, especially hyena and lion. So our camp beds should be placed away from the interior of the *zariba*, to reduce the risk of being bitten in the head or face by a hyena, whose jaws are stronger than those of a lion! The supervisor and myself collected dry branches for a fire. Soon after nightfall we were well fed and ready for a sleep. I recall falling asleep to a cacophony of sounds; the jackals seemed the noisiest.

Next morning, at about six-thirty, we were again on the move. We found ourselves picking our way through stones and dead wood which lay on the sandy floor of the Debra Wein. After about a mile or so, we were forced to stop. Ahead of us were huge boulders; and beyond them we could see black rocks. Could we somehow navigate our way through what looked like an ominous black barrier? Taking the supervisor with me, I walked ahead. The black rocks were extensive and covered the entire width of the floor of the gorge. We clambered over the rocks and continued walking for about a mile. To our astonishment we found ourselves walking in shallow water.

In Somaliland, surface water is practically unknown. Here and there, after occasional rainfall there are a few watering holes which can be used to water camels for a few weeks, but a spring which produces surface water is very rarely found. As we walked further, the water became fresher and deeper. We were amazed. The landscape beyond the black rocks seemed to offer fewer physical obstacles – and there was an apparently endless supply of fresh spring water. So we decided to attempt navigation with the Land Rover past the black rocks.

On our way back to the Land Rover we spent about two hours looking to find a way past the rocks. By the time we had decided on the most promising option, the light of day was dwindling. So rather than attempt the somewhat precarious rock-bypass in what would soon be fading light, we made camp. Our achievement that day was to have progressed only about a mile, which seemed a pitiful effort; it was in fact the result of much effort in a hot sun. I, for one, was beginning to feel the effects of fatigue. However, we looked forward to the morning with hope.

Although we slept well, I was awoken in the night by a forceful rustling in the *zariba*. Grabbing a torch, I found myself looking at the head of a striped hyena. The supervisor started shouting in a high, shrill voice. The hyena did not appreciate the combination of the torch light and the shouting. It briefly bared its teeth, growling as it did so, then turned its head and body away from the *zariba* and loped away into the darkness. Following this experience, I instituted a watchman regime; from then on, each of us would keep watch in turn for two hours during the hours of darkness.

We were up at first light to continue our journey. Over a mug of tea, I asked the Somalis whether they thought we should proceed or whether we should take the option of retracing our tracks. The response was unanimous: we were here to test the feasibility of using a route through the Debra Wein. Now it was obvious that traversing the black rocks ahead was not practicable. But when it came to the landscape on the other side, there was probably still something to be learned. In any case, looking back at the gorge with its high walls of rock and stones, what had been a reasonably easy descent could prove to be an almost impossible ascent. Without question, even though we could not know what lay ahead, we should press on. So we did.

I believe our attitude to what had turned out to be a daunting challenge could be attributed, partly at least, to our ages. I was a young man of 22; the oldest of our group was about 24. I say 'about' because most Somalis do not actually know their age. Most westerners know the year of their birth; in general Somalis do not. In any case, our youthful approach

Figure 7. North–western Somaliland, 1953, close to the border with Ethiopia. Typical landscape of a challenging, broken, stony terrain with cliffs of rock.

to life refused to accept the idea of retreat; we were strongly motivated to advance.

As we approached the rocks, we veered slowly to the right and carefully began to climb a stony hill. It may have been our imaginations, but we had the feeling that we were following the trace of a track. As we rose, we could see the giant, solid black rocks on our left. After about a quarter of a mile, the 'track' vanished. The slope of the hill became steeper and I wondered whether the Land Rover might turn over. If it did, the vehicle would slide down the scree-like surface until coming to rest on, or between, huge rocks. I asked the driver to stop. I got out below the side of the vehicle and scrambled around to the driver's side. Then I explained that I would drive over and around the hill; however, I requested the three others to stand near the front and back of the Land Rover; if the vehicle began to tip, then they should do everything possible to keep the vehicle on its four wheels by pushing against the weight.

A minute later, I was in the driver's seat and my helpers were in position. Ever so slowly, I drove the vehicle slightly upwards and around the steepest part of the hill. Now we were about 100 feet above the rocks; below, the hill looked even steeper. Every few yards I stopped for a few seconds and we would shout to one another: 'Okay?' Then the answer: 'Okay!' To traverse the hillside at a snail's pace took four hours. The Land Rover hugged the unpredictable surface for the whole distance. To my left, the black rocks were more broken; within the next mile they would die out. And we descended slowly down the scree of the hill. Soon we saw trees and, at the bottom of the hill, the water glistening in the bright sunlight. At last, we were again at the bottom of the gorge. There were boulders ahead and as we slowly continued we found water gushing through the boulders and stones. At least the black rocks were behind us.

And what lay ahead? Although we did not know, one had the impression that in the distance the gorge seemed to widen; also, the towering sides of the stony hills and cliffs seemed to be less ominous before us than those behind us. Before carrying on, I suggested we stop for an hour's rest. In the middle of the day, the sun beat down on us and the heat was exacerbated by the radiation of the nearby rocks; the slightest breeze often created a facial sensation similar to that which would be felt very close to an open iron furnace. Although we hoped the worst was behind us, the reality was that we were still trapped in the gorge.

We drove for about half a mile over the stones and found an *acacia* tree; due to their flat tops, these trees are sometimes called 'umbrella' trees. Once in the shade, we could rest: this we did for about half an hour. Certainly, I felt weary and my face and arms were burned red by the hot sun. My colleagues in the team were also fatigued; they hardly spoke. At last, I broke the silence. I explained that we had brought food for two days and we were already well into the third day. We were fortunate that, unexpectedly, we had spring water at hand. We should fill the jerry cans, each of which had a capacity of four and a half gallons. In addition, the supervisor and the helper each had a goatskin, which would also be filled.

I expressed my concern about the food problem. Used sparingly, our food could last until the evening of the following day. But after that we would have no more food. I was carrying a small .22 rifle, but we had seen no yellow-neck francolin, nor guinea fowl. In fact, since we had entered the Debra Wein we had seen virtually no sign of life, except for the nocturnal hyena.

At that precise second, I saw that we had been joined by an elderly Somali; he had appeared as though he was a spirit. In what seemed to be an uninhabited area, where had he suddenly come from? He crouched with the team as though he was one of us. He wore little more than a sort of large loincloth; simple leather sandals protected his feet. He was carrying quite a long stick, probably hewn from a tree. He was partly bald and what was left of his hair was grey. His face was relaxed and he seemed to look at us with benevolence. Then he spoke along these lines:

'I have been watching you for two days. Why did you bring that vehicle? Around here it's much easier to walk with camels. You are lucky that you have fresh water. There used to be some elephants living here, but they seem to have died out about ten years ago. They were always so happy with the water. Where are you going now?'

I asked the supervisor to find out from the old man whether the village of Bawn was far away. Suddenly, our visitor jumped up; he was looking up the side of the gorge. 'Oh my God!' he said, 'Look up there – near the top. That lion has killed one of my sheep. Look, the lion is just walking away with my sheep. Praise be to Allah! Goodbye – *Nabad Gilyo!*' Without more ado, the man rushed up the steep, stony hill, sometimes hopping from stone to stone with light agility. Now our visitor was nowhere to be seen; like a spirit, he was no more.

We carried on again. Although our progress was little more than a crawl over the stones, the main point was that we were able to continue driving in a westerly direction. After about five miles or so, we found ourselves viewing a totally different landscape. The intimidating gorge was no more. The hills on either side were becoming quite low, and what had been a relatively narrow floor of the gorge widened significantly. The water which had gushed between the rocks and boulders was now a small stream. Soon it would disappear altogether as it drained, delta-like, into the red loam of the open country which lay before us.

For the last hour of the drive that day we drove straight at the setting sun. The broken country of sandy loam was potentially ideal for locusts to breed. Especially after rain, in addition to the enlivened scrub, there would be ephemeral vegetation; so the hoppers would progress through the instars eating ravenously the whole time. Before the locusts would leave in a swarm, the countryside would be laid waste.

We stopped for the night near some *acacia* trees. We followed our usual routine, although with little to eat, we tried to strengthen ourselves with well-sugared tea. Soon, enclosed by the thorny *zariba*, we were asleep. I felt hopelessly tired; so although I could hear the cries of jackals and hyenas, I immediately slipped into a deep slumber. At the appointed hour, I would be awoken to start my stint as watchman.

The next day, although we cautiously hoped to reach the main road near Bawn, our hopes were dashed. Over a mug of sweet tea and the last of some biscuits, our driver told me that two of the Land Rover's tyres were flat. So time would be needed to repair the tubes. The tubeless tyre had not yet been developed. When the first tube was pulled from the loosened tyre, an examination showed that there would be 40 punctures to repair. The second tube was in rather better condition. In the heat of the day, the driver made the necessary repairs. As I watched him pump up the second tyre, I felt that I was watching a miracle. The driver explained that what he had done was all in a day's work. The punctures had been caused by thorns, mainly of broken boughs of *acacia* trees. He hoped for the best and he would be as careful as possible, but he would not be surprised to find a similar situation the following morning.

At last we departed on our westward course. It was about noon; the atmosphere was hot, and near what seemed to be the horizon we could see a mirage of scrub and trees. As it floated before our eyes I asked myself, with a sort of giddy sensation, whether it was, in fact, a mirage, or were my senses playing tricks on me? We pressed on till dusk, but we had still not yet reached the main road.

Just before stopping for the night, the supervisor suddenly shouted, 'Look, look! There are some guinea fowl. Allah has saved us!' I knew I had to move quickly, which I did. Within a minute, the bead of my rifle was clearly on one of the guinea fowl. I squeezed the trigger. As might happen once in 1,000 times, the cartridge did not fire. The flock of guinea fowl took off and flew for a short distance; at that point we knew the birds would race away.

Next morning we started early and continued the drive, a drive which by now had left us tired to the point of near-exhaustion, and hungry. In our plight, we were fortunate that we were not again plagued by punctures. I had already decided that should we again be immobilised by punctures, we would leave the vehicle and walk to the main road. I could not believe that the road was far away now. The Land Rover could be recovered within a day or two.

Now we were making good progress. The landscape was less broken and this allowed the driver to increase his speed to a little above 10 mph. Suddenly, the Issa helper shouted, 'Stop!' The driver stopped. The helper opened my door. 'I am sorry, we have to stop. Mr Everard, please come with me.' The helper took my arm and led me back in the direction from which we had come. 'Bend down,' he said, 'Touch the ground. What are you touching – tell me?' I bent down; the surface was hard dirt. I did not speak because I did not know what I had touched. There was a pause of perhaps half a minute. I looked at the helper. Then he spoke, 'Mr Everard, you are standing on the main road!' I felt limp. Hardly aware of the fact, I slowly walked back to our vehicle. The driver turned the Land Rover round. Now we were on the main road, and ten minutes later we had stopped in Bawn.

The driver motioned me to get out. He led me into a so-called coffee shop. In most villages throughout Somaliland, one finds at least one 'coffee shop'. In fact, these rough cafes usually offer sweet tea and sometimes simple food. The tea is mixed with camel milk, a milk that is today recognised as highly nutritious. We entered the coffee shop. As usual, the atmosphere was thick with smoke and it was quite dark. To my left, I found myself looking at a large, rectangular metal tank; steam from the boiling water rose above the tank. 'What's in there?' I asked. 'Mutton,' came the reply. I asked that the proprietor should give my team whatever they liked in the way of food. Then I grabbed a piece of meat and gnawed at it straight from the bone. The fact that I had scalded my arm barely registered in my brain.

We stayed at the coffee shop for about a half hour. Then our driver drove us back to camp. After a wash, I went to bed and, for the only time in my life, slept for a little more than

24 hours. It seemed that my basic physical system had been undermined and weakened. It would be a good two weeks before I would return to my normal energetic self.

When I did at last wake up, apart from feeling tired and the aching of my muscles, my tent seemed dark. I slipped out of my Hounsfield camp bed and looked out through the entrance flap. Our camp was under water. The watchman approached me. He explained that it had rained torrentially for the whole night; there had been long flashes of sheet lightning, accompanied by very loud, sometimes frightening, thunder. His face betrayed incredulity when I commented that I had heard nothing. At the porch of the tent the canvas veranda cover was half collapsed with the weight of rain water. This had increased the flooding effect.

When the cleaning up work was finished, the Issa helper said it would probably rain again; soon the locusts would come. He explained that the Issa always associate rain with locusts. He was right. Next day it rained again. Then, about ten days later, we began to receive reports of locusts. Soon, the mature, yellow insects would swarm over the countryside and the scouts I had positioned in likely breeding areas would report on large areas where they had seen locusts copulating; after this the females would test the wet loam or sand for softness. Then the female would penetrate the surface and lay a pod of perhaps 100 eggs, possibly even more.

With our recent experience of the Debra Wein, I positioned three scouts to the east of Bawn. From our reconnaissance, we had learned that the open, relatively flat area to the east of Bawn, between the village and the Debra Wein gorge, seemed ideal for locust breeding. Now, with the current invasion of swarms, this proved to be an area of intense and widespread infestation. The control measures would start as soon as the hoppers hatched. We were able to use motorised transport to bring in hundreds of sacks of locust bait, as well as the labourers who would spread the bait in front of the marching bands of hoppers. As the hoppers progressed through the instars they became more organised; in their gregarious state they formed huge bands. These bands devoured all forms of vegetation. Once the hoppers reached the third instar, they would form concentrations which resembled marching armies; some of the swathes of hoppers had a frontal span of up to five miles.

The reporting system followed by the scouts worked quite well. After inspection of the egg fields, dumps of locust bran were positioned nearby. Gangs of labourers were brought to the infested areas and, once the hoppers began to hatch, under the instructions of a supervisor these gangs set about their work of locating hoppers and laying the poisoned bait ahead of their march.

During the campaign, I travelled to the various areas of infestation to monitor the work. This allowed me to identify where a gang might need reinforcement or, if progress were ahead of schedule, where a gang could be moved to reinforce another. The ready supply of locust bait needed to be maintained. Depending on the size of the locust campaign, it was not unusual to employ 500 labourers, so in consequence there might well be a significant element of logistics which would need to be properly attended to.

It was during one of my monitoring rounds that I suffered an experience, the memory of which remains with me to this day. Apart from the area in the immediate vicinity of Borama and the countryside to the east and north-east, it was important not to neglect surveillance of the land to the west. I had already sketched possible routes which could be traversed by motor transport, including several *tougs* which, provided they were not in flood, could be used.

Having given much attention to the locust infestation which would need to be controlled to the north-east of Borama, I left one day to drive to a village called Gocti, which is close to the Ethiopian border. I was accompanied by the supervisor who had been my right hand man since my arrival in Borama. I also took with me the Issa helper. As was our routine, we took a jerry can of water, some rations, a jerry can of petrol and my .22 rifle, which would be used if we saw some guinea fowl or yellowneck (a francolin).

The journey initially went well. Once in Gocti, I met the local officials, after which we sat in the shade of a wall of the village police station. We had been joined by a locust scout who seemed alert and enthusiastic about his work; at that time there were no reports of locusts in the area.

While we were eating a sandwich, we heard sudden cracks of rifle shots. Fragments of mortar from the wall above us fell on and around us. At that point a police sergeant approached us.

'Sorry for the inconvenience. We use the wall for target practice,' he explained. 'Yes,' he went on, 'We have to be good shots. There are a lot of bandits around here. Once they rob someone, they just run over the border. We can't keep up with them. They are always dodging backwards and forwards. Anyway, enjoy your lunch. We will continue shooting. Nothing to worry about; the target is at least four feet above your heads. Hope there won't be a stray shot.' The sergeant laughed. Then came the next burst of rifle fire and we were showered with more mortar from the broken wall just above our heads. There was a pause, during which we quickly slipped away and left in the Land Rover.

After our abbreviated break, and feeling relieved we had not stopped a stray bullet, we headed south for a few miles, where my sketch showed us we should meet the *toug*. Soon we had descended into the wide, dry river bed. My sketch indicated that after about 20 miles of driving eastwards, we should meet the main road; this would lead us back to our camp near Borama. The first ten miles of the journey went well. The sand was quite firm and we had little difficulty negotiating the remains of dead trees and boughs which littered the floor of the *toug*.

Figure 8. Somaliland, 1953. Part of a marching band of locust nymphs, commonly called hoppers. The hoppers are about a month old and they devour all types of vegetation in their path. Such bands often have a frontage of about 5 miles (8 kilometres).

Now we were passing signs of habitation. We could see a number of women drawing water from wells. I asked the driver to skirt the wells and give them a good wide berth. We seemed to progress well. Suddenly there was a lurch; the vehicle sank a little at the back – and stopped. One of the rear wheels had sunk into what seemed to be a small, probably disused, well.

We soon found some flat wood and this was placed under a jack. The driver then began the job of jacking up the rear of the Land Rover. While this was in progress, the rest of us started gathering small pieces of dead wood; these would be placed under the rear wheels to facilitate the extraction of the wheel from the well.

Then we heard a voice. 'Who are you? What are you doing here?' We stood up and turned towards the voice. We were looking at a tall Issa tribesman who was standing near some bushes at the side of the *toug*. He was not smiling and his intense gaze was a little unnerving. The supervisor explained who we were and what we were doing. Then this strong man said, 'You have no right to be here. You are trespassers. The *toug* is reserved for our use. You should be on a road with that vehicle. You must be dealt with. I will be back with my brothers!' The man disappeared into trees and bushes. We continued our recovery work.

After about 15 minutes, the man reappeared. Now he had his brothers with him. All carried spears. The group started chanting; now they were dancing. The chanting was growing louder. The supervisor told me they were chanting in unison, 'We must kill the Outsider! We must kill the Outsider!' Feeling that the situation could become more serious and sensing that the group of Issa seemed to be working themselves into a frenzy, I decided to try and defuse the situation which was becoming more unpleasant by the second.

I advanced steadily straight at the tall leader of the group. I was relaxed and smiling. As I neared him I motioned that I would like to inspect his spear. As my hand approached the spear, the tall Issa took one step back and at the same moment raised his spear at shoulder level. His eyes were fixed on my body. Now the tip of the spear was flashing in the sunlight; and the head of the spear was rotating quickly in short bursts. My eyes were dazzled. I felt my legs sagging and my knees were banging against one another. The limit of my vision took in only the Issa with his flashing spear. A deadly silence pervaded the scene. Abruptly, the spear rotation stopped. The tribesman drew the spear back a little and gripped the shaft more tightly. Helplessly defenceless, I waited for the inevitable. There was no escape.

At that moment, a voice pierced the tense silence. It was the steady, but stern, voice of the supervisor. Afterwards he told me what he had said. 'If you touch that man, I will shoot you between the eyes. You will be dead!' With a look of dismay, the tribesman slowly lowered the spear. Now the Issa was glaring at me. I did not move. Then, when the spear was resting at the side of the Issa, I took a tentative step backwards. I did not want to turn my back on the group. After several paces backwards, I half turned. My eyes caught the eyes of the supervisor. He held my .22 rifle in his hands; he was calm and unsmiling. He beckoned me back to the Land Rover. He told me quietly that as the situation became worse, he had crept inside the Land Rover and had taken out my rifle. Then he had positioned himself at one of the vehicle's doors, from which point he could take aim at the tribesman.

Soon, the vehicle had been jacked up and the dry wood and bark were in position. The driver started the engine; and again we were en route. On our return at dusk to Borama, I gave a district officer a verbal report on the incident with the tall Issa tribesman.

At about seven o'clock on the following morning a police Land Rover stopped at our camp. A sergeant and two constables told us that they should be taken immediately to the place of the previous day's incident. Ten minutes later we were heading for the *toug*. We reached the wells and stopped.

Within a few minutes the tall Issa was shouting at us from the edge of the *toug*. One of the policemen approached the Issa. The Issa was asked whether he still wanted to kill the Outsider. Yes, he would kill the Outsider without hesitation. The Issa was then arrested, handcuffed and brought to the Land Rover.

A day later I found myself standing in front of a magistrate making my statement on what exactly had happened. After my statement had been read back to me, I was told to leave the courtroom. Through a doorway I could see the supervisor and driver, who would shortly be called as witnesses.

As I left the courtroom I found myself looking at the tall Issa; this time he was flanked by two constables of the Somali police force. Compared with his aggressive attitude of 48 hours previously, he seemed docile and sad. As I looked into his face, he showed no emotional reaction. A few days later the Issa helper mentioned that the tall Issa had been charged on three counts, including attempted murder. He had been sentenced to hard labour – for a period of three months!

With the digression behind us, we could devote all of our time to mounting the locust campaign. The work went well and most of the infestation was well controlled. After about six weeks of exhausting work, the escape of the surviving young locusts took place. The escaping locusts could barely form even a thin swarm, most of which would peter out in the following few days. Some locusts would die from poor weather conditions; most of the remainder would provide food for birds.

So our locust campaign had been a success. We had played our part in destroying the locust generation which, if the control measures had not been implemented, would have flown further south with the wind in dense swarms, leaving

Figure 9. Somaliland, 1953. A blower mounted on a truck, a mobile method used to spread locust bait ahead of marching bands of locust nymphs (hoppers). The mixture of bran and insecticide killed only the hoppers; with proper application, there were no adverse effects to humans, livestock or vegetation.

a path of devastation as far as crops and grazing were concerned. It was not an exaggeration to state that not only hunger but possible starvation had been avoided by the locust control measures.

A few days later I was told that I should prepare for a move to another area which was heavily infested with locust hoppers; the area was about 300 miles south–east of Hargeisa, the main town of Somaliland. Locally employed staff in the Borama area should be paid off, after which the supervisor and myself, with our driver, should travel to Hargeisa; I was expected there within the week. After receiving a briefing at the locust control headquarters, I would be prepared for my next locust control assignment.

Before leaving for Hargeisa about five days later, I made a few farewell courtesy calls. One of these was to the district commissioner's office. After a short chat and farewell hand-shake, I left the office complex by a side door. As I stepped into the sunlight, I heard a shout. Then I saw a tall, muscular man take a few steps towards me; then he seemed to jerk and stop. It was the tall Issa. I approached him; he smiled and shook my hand. Then I noticed a metal bracket around his ankle, to which was attached a chain.

I sat with the Issa tribesman for several minutes. The smile on his face faded; now he looked thoughtful and a little sad. Then he spoke through an interpreter: 'I am sorry. I am very sorry. I didn't mean to kill you. We got carried away. If you need a watchman, I will look after you and your belongings. No one will dare to come near me. You don't need to pay me. But if each day I could have a ration of rice and dates, I will be happy.'

I explained to the tribesman that I would be leaving the following day. I hoped that after serving his sentence he would return to his clan and live peacefully. A glimmer of a smile crossed his face. Then he said, 'May Allah bless you. Praise be to Allah. *Nabad Gilyo* – Goodbye.'

The next day, we left for Hargeisa.

4

The Ogaden

Hargeisa is the main town of Somaliland. Certainly in the 1950s, one might hesitate to call Hargeisa a 'capital city'. The centre of the town was a disorganised cluster of buildings; otherwise there existed a sprawling mass of semi-permanent hut-like dwellings, which housed the population of several hundred thousand. Most of these dwellings were called *gurghis*; a *gurghi* is a temporary house usually used by nomads. The *gurghi* consists of hooped, flexible wooden rods which support carpet-like matting. Sometimes dried mud was spread over weaker points to improve protection from inclement weather. The *gurghi* is ideal as a transportable dwelling. If, for example, a nomadic family needs to move to a better grazing area, then little time is lost in dismantling the *gurghi*; then the hoops and matting are loaded onto camels, ready for the move. In Somaliland, it is a common sight to see a caravan – perhaps a line of ten or 12 burden camels – each carrying a *gurghi*.

Hargeisa was named the main town of Somaliland in 1941, at the end of the military campaign during which British forces evicted the Italian administration. In the 1930s, Somaliland had become part of what Italy called Italian East Africa. Before Hargeisa became the main town, Berbera, as a strategic port on the Gulf of Aden, was the main town. Great Britain had

had connections with Somaliland since the end of the nineteenth century. In fact, in 1888 a Treaty was agreed between Great Britain and the Somali tribes under which the British were permitted to reside in Berbera for trading purposes; the Treaty also included the right to defend British interests in the area, both on land and at sea.

I would like to offer a little more explanation concerning the more recent history of Hargeisa. In 1960 (a few years after the subject of this book), the Somali Republic came into being. At that time, the new State comprised the former Italian Trusteeship of Somalia, together with the former Somaliland Protectorate (usually referred to as Somaliland). In 1960, the capital of the new State was Mogadishu. During the ensuing years, the Somali Republic became increasingly politically fragmented. Now, we have Puntland, Somaliland and so forth. During the period covered by this book (the 1950s), Somaliland was a separate country to Somalia. At that time Hargeisa was the main town of Somaliland. And today Hargeisa, after the fragmentation of the Somali Republic with Mogadishu as its capital, finds itself again as the capital city of Somaliland.

Hargeisa naturally housed the seat of government and hosted the headquarters of a number of organisations and commercial enterprises. The headquarters of the Desert Locust Control (DLC) was situated about seven miles from the town.

The DLC headquarters had been used during the war as a munitions dump. There were several rectangular single-storey buildings which had been used to store munitions; the appearance of the buildings was characterless. Each of these buildings was surrounded by an absorptive wall of grey, loose stones which had been heaped to the height of the building. Inside, each building had been adapted for residential or office use. In addition, there was a large hangar-like shed to store and repair DLC vehicles; these were mainly Land Rovers and Dodge Power Wagons.

The entire camp area was stony and practically bereft of vegetation. There were, however, two redeeming features. One was the fact that most days in Hargeisa were sunny days and with an altitude of over 4,000 feet above sea level, humidity was pleasantly low. The other feature was that locust control work was, literally, a full-time job; so boredom, or perhaps unhappiness with the stony working environment, rarely arose as a factor. One was simply too busy.

My briefing in the Hargeisa DLC base lasted three days. The senior field officer described the current locust situation throughout the country. He explained exactly where locust swarms from the Arabian peninsula had crossed the coast, as well as the areas in which breeding was taking place. He went on to say that breeding was also occurring further south. In particular, widespread locust campaigns were already in progress in the Ogaden province of Ethiopia. Perhaps these locusts had already laid their egg pods in the north; so now the swarms had been carried southwards on the monsoon wind and, before dying, the females had again laid egg pods.

The senior field officer emphasised that the breeding in the Ogaden was heavy. He wanted me to strengthen the effort. One of the locust control officers was based in a camp a few miles from a village called Jin'Ali. The locust campaign was already well underway. I should travel to Jin'Ali, familiarise myself with the campaign in progress and, as soon as possible, take over the reins. The man already in position would then be released to take up duties elsewhere. He asked me to leave within three days. Before departing, I should spend time with the transport section, the accounts office and so forth.

Before the senior field officer shook my hand and wished me *bon voyage,* seemingly as an afterthought he mentioned that the Ogaden was not the safest place in the world. So it would be a good idea to report at police stations en route and ask them if they had any special advice regarding personal security.

During my briefing, the head accountant explained that the nearest bank to Jin'Ali was about 100 miles distant, in a small town called Las Anod. So I was given some cash to meet immediate needs. I was also handed a cheque; to cash the cheque, I would need to travel to Las Anod. The cash would be needed to pay the labourers, who received their pay and rations every two weeks.

Having followed instructions, on the evening of the second day in Hargeisa the Land Rover I was to use was packed up with water, spare petrol, rations and my belongings. As insects seemed to assume they could invade my clothes and settle down, I had asked a carpenter to make a sturdy box for my personal effects. The box was well packed and duly loaded. A driver had been introduced to me; from the outset he was unfailingly helpful.

On the journey to Jin'Ali there were two stops. As we travelled southwards towards the first stop, which was a town called Awareh, we found ourselves driving through a swarm of locusts; the locusts were yellow in colour and many were breeding. About two hours later we reached Awareh. The police superintendent welcomed me and said he would send a message to Hargeisa to report my arrival; a second message would be sent to Danot, to say that I was en route. I asked him to send a further message to the locust control headquarters in Hargeisa. My message read along the following lines:

> From Everard. En route to Awareh today, traversed at mile 53 swarm of mature yellow locusts for six miles. Copulating hard.

The superintendent told me he would transmit the message by Morse code, since radio communication had encountered a fault. Then he asked me to call on a Mr Aske, who was responsible for administering the area.

Mr Aske was a charming man. He invited me to his house for a meal; the main course was a perfectly cooked gazelle steak. He would take the opportunity to tell me about the Ogaden. He had seen service in the Sudan and used a title from former days – *Bimbashi,* which meant leader of a thousand men. In fact, *Bimbashi* was a rank used in the Turkish army in the days of the Ottoman Empire; it roughly corresponded to a military major or colonel.

Mr Aske explained that, historically, the Ogaden had become part of Ethiopia after the conquest of the ruler Menelik II, in the latter part of the nineteenth century. Since the sixteenth century a substantial part of the then Abyssinia had been part of an Islamic Sultanate. Menelik's aim was to reverse the situation, which he managed to do.

During the Italian campaign of the mid-1930s, Abyssinia had become, together with Somalia, a part of Italian East Africa; this also included Eritrea, to the north of Abyssinia. However, by 1941, Italian East Africa had ceased to exist because the British had launched a military campaign to oust the Italians. By the end of the 1940s, Somaliland was under the administration of the British, while the former Italian Somalia was administered by the Italians. Somaliland was called a Protectorate, while Somalia had the status of a UN-mandated Trusteeship.

Now Mr Aske came to the heart of a political problem, namely, the Ogaden. The Ogaden was quite a large province of what was now called Ethiopia; geographically, the Ogaden covered an area of about 200,000 square kilometres. In contrast to most of the rest of Coptic Christian Ethiopia, almost all the inhabitants were Muslim Somalis. A few years previously, after the dissolution of Italian East Africa, the British had proposed that the province should become part of the so-called Greater Somalia. The proposal was well received, until the Americans decided to support Ethiopia's claim to retain the province; at that point, the British proposal died. So now Coptic Christian Ethiopia found itself with a large province in the south east which was inhabited by Muslim Somalis, This was, of course, a total mismatch.

Although the Ogaden was an Ethiopian province, under a recent treaty the adjacent area to the south of the Somaliland Protectorate was to be administered for a few years by the British; in effect, it was a sort of buffer zone. This area, which extended for about 50 miles, was called the *Haud; Haud* is the Somali word for south. In effect, the *Haud* was administered almost as part of Somaliland.

Finally, Mr Aske explained that my destination, Jin'Ali, was a village situated in the *Haud* area. This meant that if I needed support in some way, then I should contact the nearest representative of the British administration. This would be the administration in Las Anod or Danot, some 100 or 150 miles away. He said that the next town to the south of Jin'Ali was Galadi, which was in fact a border town on the Ethiopian side. Galadi was some 30 miles to the south of Jin'Ali.

Before wishing me Godspeed, Mr Aske told me that the entire *Haud* was vulnerable to attacks from *shifta*; this was a word used for bandits. The *Haud* was a relatively lawless area. As far as the *shifta* were concerned, they could attack and rob in the *Haud*; afterwards they could quickly escape over a border, either into Ethiopia or Somalia.

The following morning we left for the only real town between Awareh and my destination; the town was called Danot. There, I reported to the police station. The super-intendent had already been told I would call on him. He was a matter-of-fact man and apparently busy. He told me he would send a message to Hargeisa to confirm my arrival. Then he handed me a message he had received from the locust control headquarters in Hargeisa. The message read,

For Everard. Your message re. locust swarm received. Please, stop copulating and kill the locusts.

Where would our world be without humour?

After I had pocketed the message, the unsmiling super-intendent stated that for the duration of my stay in Jin'Ali he wanted to assure my personal protection. Therefore, two armed members of the Haud Police Force were waiting to leave with me; the senior man held the rank of corporal. Both were from the Issa tribe. They were entirely at my disposal and I should feel reassured that they would constantly provide excellent personal security. A significant advantage in employing police in that area from the Issa tribe was that the Issa had little affinity with the tribesmen in the Ogaden; so in the event that we might meet trouble, we could rest assured that the Issa would show no sympathy with the tribes of the Ogaden.

Dressed in their discreet, dark blue uniforms, complete with puttees and heavy black shoes, the policemen looked in top physical condition; with their quietly confident, down-to-earth disposition, one's feeling of security could only be enhanced. And, after all, these men were Issa, a tribe respected for their bravery.

The roads in the *Haud* were sandy, with occasional fine stony patches. After recent rain, the vegetation of low bushes and *acacia* trees looked fresh; sometimes, one could see small, colourful ephemeral plants between the bushes. At sunset I arrived in Jin'Ali and was directed to the locust control camp some seven miles further along the sandy road. There I met the locust control officer, who lost no time in describing the status of the locust campaign in progress. He explained that the hoppers were already in the third and fourth instars. The marching, devouring hopper bands covered a large area of the bush; so much effort would be needed to kill as many of the hoppers as possible in order to reduce the size of the escape. Only three or four weeks remained before the surviving locusts would swarm and fly away.

Before the locust officer left, he did his best to familiarise me with all aspects of the campaign in progress. He had employed about 350 labourers to spread locust bait. Within the camp area, about a dozen Dodge Power Wagons were parked, and these were used to deliver sacks of bait to the various areas of infestation. The locust camp was large and sections were reserved for vehicles, 40-gallon drums of petrol, a huge dump of sacks of locust bait, about ten 40-gallon galvanised drums of water, as well as domestic quarters. The latter consisted of tents and a hut-like room constructed of dried boughs, dried mud and grass; this room was used as the office and for the locust officer's meals.

A few days before his departure, the locust control officer said he would give the labourers their pay and rations; these consisted of dates and rice. He explained that the next pay day would be due in two weeks' time. Now that the money side had been organised, my colleague prepared to depart.

On the eve of his departure, over dinner, my colleague explained one last point. He had forgotten to mention that a few days previously, one of the drivers had misbehaved himself in the Ethiopian border town of Galadi. The man in question had been sent with three labourers in a Dodge Power Wagon to Galadi. The Wagon carried seven empty 40-gallon water drums. Approaching the town, the Wagon needed to pass through an Ethiopian immigration and customs post. There, the load of supposedly empty water drums had been inspected; and it was found that one drum was full of ghee. Ghee is a type of clarified butter used for cooking. By not paying customs duty, the driver had intended selling the ghee in the market place at the normal market price. Having bought the ghee in Somaliland free of duty, the driver anticipated a profit of about 25 per cent.

The current status of the affair was that the driver was sitting in a prison cell and the Wagon had been impounded. The locust control officer had received a message that he should not travel to Galadi to discuss resolution of the issue; all officials had been instructed not to talk to him. In addition, the supply of fresh water from the Galadi wells had been suspended indefinitely.

My colleague told me that the amount of water currently available would last about three days. He had made enquiries about another possible source to buy water; so far, no alternative water supply source had been found. So, unless the problem could be overcome within three days, then the camp would need to be dismantled and the locust campaign abandoned.

On this unhappy note, the following day my colleague wished me good luck and departed. Suddenly, I was responsible for a widespread locust campaign which was only four weeks from reaching a critical stage: that is to say, before the surviving locusts would swarm and fly south, the so-called escape. And the end of our water supply was in sight!

An hour later a driver was transporting me, with an interpreter Somali/English/Amharic, to Galadi. The 30-mile drive over stones and potholes took three hours. At the border post I stated I had come to pay a courtesy call on the governor. Near the centre of the town I was directed to a fort-like building. At the entrance I stated that I wished to call on the governor. Two armed soldiers accompanied me up two flights of stone stairs. Before an imposing door, I was asked to wait. Three minutes later a smart, handsome, clean-shaven young captain of the Ethiopian army walked towards me and shook my hand; he was relaxed and smiling. This was the governor of the area.

Like most well-educated Amharas, the captain spoke good French with a perfect pronunciation. The meeting in the governor's office lasted not more than ten minutes. The governor had been apprised of the illegal ghee problem. I should not worry. The locust infestation was much more important; the locust control problem demanded my full attention. In the circumstances, the driver would be fined, the Wagon would be released within 24 hours and, most important, the fresh, precious well-water of Galadi would be available for us for as long as it was needed. All he asked of me was that I should have the water drums checked at the time they crossed the border to make sure they were empty!

Having thanked the governor, I rose to leave. However, the governor walked around his desk, took my arm and announced we would have lunch together in the town; the main dish would be *zigeny*, an Ethiopian dish that was hotter on the tongue than the hottest curry anyone reading this may have eaten! During the meal the governor frequently offered me wine or beer; and it was not long before this happy man told me his life story.

He explained he had, unfortunately, shown poor judgement a couple of years previously. He had fallen in love with a General's wife, and the affair had been discovered! The result was that he would spend the rest of his military career in Galadi. I asked him why he was such a seemingly happy man. Well, he responded, Galadi was regarded as the worst punishment station in Ethiopia. So he was comforted that life could not become even more unpleasant. Therefore he was a happy man!

During the lunch, on a more serious note, the governor explained that military control over the area generally was very limited. The Ogaden was a lawless area and when Ethiopian military units had tried to extend control a few kilometres outside of the Galadi township, they were often ambushed, with soldiers being killed. So his present policy was that all military units should stay in the town's barracks.

Before I bade farewell to the young governor, he explained that armed bandits were commonplace in the Ogaden. Most of their rifles stemmed from the war years of the 1930s: in other words, most of the rifles had been stolen and sold after the British military campaign had been mounted to evict the Italians from the Ogaden and beyond.

With the water supply problem resolved, I lost no time during the ensuing days in progressing the widespread, and intensive, locust campaign. This was now a race against time. The escaping locust swarm had to be reduced to the absolute minimum.

Each day we rose between five and six and worked hard till sunset. Then, with the aid of a Tilley kerosene lamp, there were administrative matters which needed attention. Once these had been dealt with, it was time for a quick dinner, followed by bed. Each morning I was awoken with a mug of tea brought to my tent, which adjoined the hut-like room. The tea would be placed on the wooden box which contained my belongings. I could simply stretch out my arm and grab the mug which was resting on the box. Within five minutes I would be up and ready to start my working day.

In addition to the efforts in progress in the locust infested areas and together with organising the supporting logistical needs of the campaign, constant surveillance had to be maintained over yet more possible breeding areas. For this purpose scouts were employed to patrol defined areas. For this particular campaign, some 14 scouts were employed. These men often had previous experience at spotting possible breeding areas and, with a practised eye, were skilful in assessing potential breeding grounds. Sometimes they would dig shallow holes in search of egg pods. Typically, the scouts would return to our camp once, perhaps twice, a week. Apart from telling us where they had patrolled, sometimes they brought egg pods as evidence of what they had found.

Of all the scouts who participated in supporting our work, two men, in particular, seemed to be at odds with the rest of the team. These two apparently worked together. One was tall and looked very strong; the other was of medium height and build. After they had come to see me three times in one week, I questioned whether, in fact, they were patrolling the area which had been designated. If they had been patrolling as instructed, then I was at a loss to understand how they could do their job properly and find time to return to our camp with the latest information. How could they cover the distance three times in one week? They responded that they performed their duties assiduously and wanted me to have up-to-date locust breeding information; they told me that, if necessary, they would walk half the night to reach our camp in a timely way. The matter ended there, although if I had not been constantly busy, I might perhaps have wondered a little longer.

To assure coordination, once or twice a week I sat down with the three or four supervisors who were directing the work in the various areas of infestation. It was at one of these meetings that the senior supervisor mentioned that the workers would need to be paid in the next two or three days. Those who were working within ten miles of our base could walk to our camp to receive their pay and rations; those who worked further afield would be asked to come to particular points where they would be paid.

The supervisor understood that I would need to travel to Las Anod to collect money. I confirmed that this was correct. We could leave for Las Anod early the following morning; if all went well, we would return the following evening. The day after, I could pay the workers. None of them were literate, so they would sign with a thumbprint against their names. Each sheet of the payroll was signed by myself and countersigned by a witnessing supervisor.

The following morning we drove northwards to Bohotleh, which is a village on the border with Somaliland. By about one o'clock we were in Las Anod. The small town is situated on a vast plain of gypsum rock. All seemed quiet. On arrival at the bank I found the door closed. Our banging on the door awoke the watchman. Still sleepy, the man told us that the previous day had been the day of prayers. Today was a holiday. The next day was also a holiday. So if we needed something from the bank, it would be a good idea to return in three days' time. Having made his suggestion, the man returned to a shallow mattress; he pulled a blanket over his head and seemed instantly to resume his slumber.

Having called on the district commissioner in his house, and having been courteously told there would be no possibility of cashing my cheque for at least two days, we felt we had no option but to return to our camp, 100 miles away. We arrived in Jin'Ali a little after dusk. After a bowl of soup and a cup of tea, I went to bed.

Early next morning the routine was followed and the cook's help brought a mug of tea. But on this particular morning the routine could not be followed. He woke me up and asked where he should put the tea. My sleepy response was short – he should put it on the box, as usual. His reply was short, calm and to the point. There was no box!

I sprang out of bed and took hold of a torch. I walked outside the hut and shone the torchlight at the outside of my tent. The two protecting policemen were asleep on the ground. They woke up. I led them into my tent. The corporal took the torch from my hand and shone the light on the sand, which was my floor. The light showed clearly large footprints. And what was next to the footprints? There, clearly imprinted in the sand, was the brass butt of a rifle. The corporal praised Allah that I had not been awoken by the intruder. I would have been instantly shot!

Ten minutes later, the Issa policemen were following the footprints in the sand; both policemen were armed. The footprints led them to where the intruders had broken the perimeter of our camp, the *zariba* of camel thorn bush. I accompanied the policemen for about an hour. The sun was rising and I knew it would soon become hot. The policemen were still following footprints, although now they were moving ever faster; sometimes they seemed to put in short sprints. The policemen were running steadily. I then decided to let these extremely fit men continue on their own; sweating profusely, I was wearing the only piece of clothing I possessed – a green silk dressing gown which had been given to me by my father as a *bon voyage* present on the day I had left England for Africa.

Just as I stopped to retrace my steps, two rifle shots rang out. The corporal motioned me to crouch behind a bush. A few seconds later, he and the constable were running in the direction of the shots. I waited in the sand behind the bush. Then I heard more shots; this time there were several. I waited. And I wondered what might happen next. Would the constables return? What would happen if they had been killed or wounded? Would the *shifta* find me; or would they make good their escape? As I crouched, sweating, behind the bush, these thoughts flooded through my mind.

To my relief, after about 15 minutes the policemen came into view. The policemen had caught up with the *shifta;* they were dividing my belongings between them. Shots had been exchanged. There were two *shifta;* one was a tall man and the other a man of medium height. A shot from the constable had passed through the clothes of one of the *shifta*, whereupon the man had dropped some of my clothes and a small amount of money. Then the *shifta* had fled.

Back at our camp, I consulted with the senior supervisor and the policemen. From the description of the *shifta*, it was agreed that they were locust scouts and we soon deduced that they were the pair who frequently had visited, and re-visited, the camp, supposedly with locust breeding information; in fact, they had been familiarising themselves with the lay-out of the office and my tent. The name of the taller man was Warsameh Deria. We then concluded that the pair believed that my box contained the cash which I had hoped to collect the previous day in Las Anod. They had no knowledge that my journey to Las Anod had been in vain.

The corporal asked me to accompany him to Jin'Ali, where we would meet the Elders. An hour later, after the corporal

Figure 10. Ogaden Province, Ethiopia, 1953. Somali bandits – Somali:
shifta. *Most weapons used by the* shifta *had been seized from Italian*
military stores during the war with Abyssinia in the 1930s.

had recounted the armed robbery to the Elders, the corporal
told them that all my belongings must be returned to me
within 48 hours; otherwise the Elders should expect consequences. The Elders responded this would be unlikely.
Warsameh Deria was well known and had probably fled over
the Ethiopian border. They knew his village and would do
their best to comply.

With no apparent result, two days later we were driving
again to Jin'Ali. This time, the corporal picked up an Elder
and our group was driven to the village of Warsameh Deria.
At the request of the corporal, we were followed by two
Dodge Power Wagons.

After making enquiries in the small village, the corporal approached me with a man and a young woman. He explained that the woman was the sister of Warsameh Deria and the man was a brother-in-law. In the absence of information about the whereabouts of Warsameh Deria, both of these relations were under arrest. Then he instructed that their *gurghis* should be dismantled and the rods and matting should be loaded on to the Wagons. He then stated that all sheep and goats of the village should be rounded up and brought to our camp.

Before departing, the corporal called the Elder who had travelled with us, together with two Elders of the village. He told them the man, woman and livestock would be enclosed in a *zariba* next to our camp. The man and woman would receive a daily water ration; that was all. The livestock would not be fed, but might be watered.

The Elders protested that the situation was not within their control. The corporal was unmoved. He listened briefly before turning to me to say we should return to our camp. There the additional *zariba* was cut and put in place. Within hours, the man, woman and hundreds of livestock, 584 in all, would find themselves enclosed within a sort of prison camp; it was bound to be hot and there would be little water for them.

The next morning I visited the overcrowded enclosure. Most of the animals were resting and many seemed listless. The woman seemed to be asleep near the edge of the *zariba*. She had a fine face; at the same time, she looked frail and her face expressed hopelessness. I asked to talk to the corporal: I gave him my opinion that this was not the place to hold the woman; I asked him to release her. Even though the incentive to produce my belongings might be nullified, I felt the inhuman way in which the woman was being treated could never be justified. Eventually, the corporal agreed and the woman was released. Then the corporal spoke to the man.

He told him to find Warsameh Deria and organise the return of my belongings. If this did not happen, then the livestock would die.

Once the woman and man had been released, the corporal asked for a meeting with me and the senior supervisor. The corporal explained that, in his opinion, my life would be in danger on a daily basis. The *shifta* would lose no time in trying to avenge themselves. From that moment the corporal would accompany me at all times, especially when I left the camp. In his judgement, the sooner I could leave the area the better.

On the next day I visited all the main areas where locust control efforts were in progress. The control work was going well. In any case, the work would reach its natural conclusion in about ten or 12 days, when the escaping adult locusts would swarm and fly southwards.

Over the next few days, I systematically reduced our control resources. A number of vehicles, each laden with tentage, tarpaulins, water drums and other equipment were returned to Hargeisa. My plan was to finally leave about a week later. Now I concentrated our control efforts in two areas which had been very strongly infested with hoppers. A final mopping up operation was needed. I would then close the campaign. At that time, I would finally pay the wages of all the labourers and others who had worked so hard to successfully control the infestation.

After a last visit of the worst affected areas, I returned to our camp. There, I organised the trip to Las Anod. My plan was to stay in Las Anod overnight. The following morning I would cash the cheque and return to Jin'Ali. Then all the cash proceeds of the cheque could be used the same day for the wages; so by nightfall my cash holding would be virtually zero.

The next day I was returning with the corporal from Jin'Ali. Because of the heat, we were driving in an open Land Rover.

As we drove towards the camp, I noticed a man standing on the side of the road. He stood, motionless, in the shade of a 20-foot high termite hill; termite hills were a common feature throughout the region. As we passed the man, there was a quick movement of his arms and within a second he had hurled a spear at my head; my reactions are good, but the incident happened so quickly, I had no time to react. The spear passed at lightning speed a little behind my head. At that point I did react; I accelerated hard to escape the attacker.

About ten seconds later the corporal touched my arm. He asked me to stop and turn the vehicle round because he wanted to arrest the attacker. With apprehension, I followed his instructions and drove through the bush. Within minutes we had caught up with the attacker. The corporal jumped out of the Land Rover and chased the man, whom he arrested. He led the man back to the Land Rover and quietly told him to climb into the back of the vehicle. The man refused. A second later the man was lying unconscious over the tail gate of the Land Rover; one blow from the corporal had rendered the man unconscious. The corporal lifted the man's legs into the back of the vehicle. Then the corporal turned to me and, in his calm but firm way, told me the man would be charged with attempted murder. Now we could return to our camp. I never saw the man again.

Arriving at our camp, we found a group of Elders standing near the entrance to my hut-like office; there were also two constables. The corporal explained he had sent a message to Danot for reinforcements. From that night I would have 24-hour protection; two constables would be on duty by day and two by night.

I received the Elders. Apart from an interpreter, I asked that the senior supervisor and corporal should be present. The meeting was brief. After presenting me with a young goat as a sign of peace, the Elders stated that they had done their best to find Warsameh Deria, but without success.

They said they had done what was asked of them, albeit without result. Now they asked the police to honour their side of the agreement. In short, the livestock should be released immediately. The corporal responded this was out of the question. On my behalf, he thanked the Elders for the goat. He then requested the Elders to leave the camp. Looking gravely desolate, the Elders retreated.

After making arrangements for the locust labourers to be paid the following day, I left for Las Anod, arriving just after sunset. There I called on the district commissioner. He invited me to stay the night in his house. Early the next day I cashed the cheque and drove back to Jin'Ali. Without delay, the waiting labourers were paid off. Those in the more outlying areas were also paid. At sunset, with practically all the money disbursed, we returned to our camp.

I then called the supervisors and the corporal for a short meeting. After thanking them all for their splendid efforts, I told them that with the locust campaign successfully completed, we should prepare to leave Jin'Ali. The remaining Dodge Power Wagons should depart the following morning; they would be loaded with residual materials and equipment. This would leave the two Land Rovers. We could leave at about 4.30 in the afternoon and drive through the night to Danot. It was obviously important that the plan should remain secret.

Next day, the first part of the plan went smoothly and the loaded Wagons left by ten o'clock. The camp was now an empty space, except for the Land Rovers. In an adjacent *zariba* the livestock remained enclosed. With their minimum intake of water, many of the animals looked thin and listless; they made practically no noise.

At about midday I noticed two men who were standing near the entrance of the *zariba*. As they approached, I recognised one of the Elders; he was accompanied by a young man of about 20. Suddenly, two constables were at my side;

each was holding a rifle. The Elder said he had come with a simple message. At last, contact had been made with the *shifta*. My clothes would be returned to me. However, to avoid identification of the *shifta*, I should walk to a certain destination and wait in a clearing at midnight. When I would reach the clearing, my belongings would be returned. The young man who accompanied the Elder would guide me to the clearing. The walk to the destination would take about two and a half hours. The Elder shook my hand, bade me farewell and left.

My first question was to the corporal. Did he think this was a trap? Was this the last chance to kill me? The corporal acknowledged the risk. He nevertheless thought the offer was genuine. The condition of the livestock was deteriorating and its owners were desperate to regain the animals which represented most of their assets. Also, the Elders wanted to demonstrate that they had power and authority to resolve the problem.

If I had been in my 30s or 40s, then I believe that I would have decided to cut my losses and leave for Danot as planned later in the day. I also had a feeling that the corporal, too, wanted to show that he knew how to get results. In any case, at the age of 22, I decided to accept the offer.

The senior supervisor and myself, accompanied by the corporal and two constables, left our camp with the guide at about nine o'clock in the evening. There was no moon, but the clear, starlit heavens lightened the darkness. We walked in single file on the firm sand. I found myself in the middle of the file; ahead of me and behind a constable seemed to keep me under safety surveillance. In the early stages of the walk our guide followed a camel track, but after an hour or so he left the path and led us through the low bush, as though he was following a straight line. I had expected to hear the cries of animals like jackals or hyenas. In fact, except for the occasional whispered exchange between our group, all was quiet.

Now one gradually picked out hump-like forms silhouetted in the darkness. The guide stopped. He whispered that we had arrived. The forms were *gurghis* of a small village. The clearing was nearby. All remained quiet; apparently, the villagers were asleep. Our guide led us away slightly from the nearest *gurghi*; after perhaps 50 yards, he stopped. He told us we had reached the designated clearing.

I looked at my watch and with difficulty read the time. It was 11.30. I suggested to the corporal that the constables could make a short reconnaissance around the clearing to seek out signs of life. I had in mind that *shifta* might be preparing for an attack at midnight. The constables returned about 20 minutes later. They had patrolled the area around the clearing; there was no sign of life. Then I told the corporal I would enter the clearing at midnight. I suggested that the constables should take up firing positions at about 45 degrees to my right and left. If there was gunfire, they should shoot at the source.

Crouching by a bush in the sand with the corporal, I waited for five minutes. Then I stood up and walked into the clearing. After about 20 yards, I stopped. I waited in the dark silence. Turning my head, I could make out silhouettes of bushes. Looking up, the stars were sparkling in the heavens. I knew I was an easy, defenceless target. At the same time, I did not feel afraid.

Having waited in the silence for about five minutes, I concluded that nothing would happen. Just as I had turned to retreat, I heard a sound on the other side of the clearing. I stopped. Within a few seconds I could make out the form of a person. The form approached. Now a tall, hooded man was standing in front of me; his hands were placed across his chest and he was carrying something. The hands dropped and I heard what seemed like a bundle, which fell quietly on to the sand below. The man turned around and he walked away into the darkness. I bent down and I could feel a blanket wrapped around something soft. I carried the bundle back to the edge of the clearing, where the corporal relieved me of the bundle. Then we started our ten-mile walk back to our camp.

Later, at about three o'clock in the morning we examined the contents of the blanket by torchlight. The blanket contained most of my missing clothes. Separately, in a small knotted cloth, some of the cash I had been given for small purchases had been returned. So this particular mission had been accomplished.

At first light the next day the sheep and goats were returned to the owners who, apparently, knew of the return of my belongings and were waiting at the camp entrance. As soon as the livestock had been taken away, the corporal told me it was important that we should all leave soon. Now that the *shifta* had nothing to lose, we could be attacked and murdered at any time.

At two o'clock that day we were about to leave. The Land Rovers had been loaded and we were ready to depart. I had a sudden thought. Where was the goat? It was a nice animal and on two or three evenings I had even taken it for short walks on a string. The goat was nowhere to be seen. Then I looked into one or two twinkling eyes of the supervisor, the drivers of the Land Rovers and the constables. Their smiles gave way to laughter. Yes, the goat had been sacrificed; and my colleagues felt all the better for their feast.

We left a little later than planned and at first we were slowed by the deteriorating condition of the road. By about three in the afternoon the heat of the day gradually began to subside. Now we were travelling quite slowly on the pot-holed road. I began to muse a little on the challenges of the completed locust control campaign, laced as it had been with the dangerous interventions of the *shifta*.

I was suddenly jerked out of my musings by the crack of a rifle shot. The corporal was lying on tentage in the back of the

Land Rover. In contrast to his reaction in the spear incident, he told the driver to accelerate away from the danger, which he did. Would this be the final incident? A few miles down the road the driver stopped. He inspected the wing on my side of the Land Rover. The bullet hole told its own story. The bullet had passed through the vehicle's wing, a little above my knees.

In Danot the police bade me *adieu*. The corporal said he was sorry that we had been sometimes exposed to *shifta* activity, although this was regarded in the Ogaden as normal. He wished us well for the future. On the following day we left for Awareh, after which we travelled to Hargeisa. Now I had to prepare for my next assignment.

About 18 months later, after work periods in Ethiopia and Eritrea, I was appointed as the senior field officer in Somaliland; now I took responsibility for locust control operations throughout the country. On one of my field inspection trips, I needed to pass through the village of Jin'Ali.

As we approached the village, I found it almost impossible to control my feeling of apprehension, almost fear. If the driver stopped at a coffee shop and I were to find myself face-to-face with Warsameh Deria, how would he react? The driver duly stopped and disappeared into what was really a roadside café. He soon reappeared in the doorway and beckoned me inside.

With hesitation and a thumping heart I made for the doorway. I entered. Looking around, to my relief there was no sign of Warsameh Deria. I was handed a cup of sweet tea. By now I had learned to speak fluent Somali. I talked a little with my neighbour. Then I addressed the proprietor. I wondered whether he had heard the name Warsameh Deria? The proprietor's response was short and to the point. Warsameh Deria was a terrible man. He had a lot of blood on his hands! Last year the *shifta* had been shot and killed. Praise be to Allah!

The German Brockhaus Encyclopaedia contains an article on the Ogaden. At the end of the article, the following passage has been included:

> The hostile mistrust of the inhabitants, the enjoyment they derive from robbery and murder, effectively closes the area to Europeans. (*The Unknown Horn Of Africa*, J.L. James, 1888.)

Yes, indeed!

5

Stones

A t the end of 1954, shortly after my 24th birthday, I received a letter from the director of the Desert Locust Control (DLC), Philip Stephenson, in which he appointed me as the senior field officer of the Desert Locust Control for Eritrea and northern Ethiopia. Two weeks later I found myself sitting in a well-appointed office at the DLC headquarters in Asmara, Eritrea.

The city of Asmara is situated at an altitude of almost 8,000 feet above sea level and its general appearance bore many of the physical characteristics of a typical Italian provincial town. The wide, paved thoroughfares were lined with robust-looking palm trees, behind which elegant shops displayed beautiful clothes, shoes and other luxuries. Interspersed within the large shopping area were bars and restaurants, in front of which guests sat at tables covered with colourful table cloths; above them, brightly coloured umbrellas protected them from the rays of a hot sun which streamed through the thin, high-altitude air. The traffic was well regulated and such buildings as the town hall, the opera house, and the cathedral were formidably impressive. If one drove to the outskirts of the city, sometimes one drove along avenues of eucalyptus trees. Naturally, for a locust field officer who had become accustomed to life in the semidesert of the

Horn of Africa, the apparent unreality of Asmara represented something of a culture shock.

For the first few weeks of what would be an unexpectedly short tenure of office in my newly appointed position, I studied all available reports of migratory movements of locusts, as well as the areas where locust breeding had occurred. Within the complex picture which emerged, I concluded that one large area of potential interest was what was loosely described as the Takazze Valley. I found numerous reports of locust movements within parts of the Takazze Valley; in addition, I found reports of locust swarms having been seen above the higher, mountainous areas which were close to the Takazze river. In particular, reports from the large town of Gondar, which lies at an altitude of 2,100 metres (7,000 feet) above sea level in the Lake Tana area, described large locust swarms flying southwards. Probably, these swarms had crossed the Red Sea from Arabia. However, up to that time, in early 1955, no member of the DLC had made a reconnaissance in the Takazze Valley to verify the numerous reports of locust activity; so these reports were, in basic terms, second hand.

Although the Takazze river is not part of the major river systems which traverse Ethiopia, nevertheless it is a significant river which flows through both high mountains and, at a lower altitude, towards the Sudanese and Eritrean borders. The lower-altitude scrub land through which the Takazze river flows as it descends towards Sudan would, typically, be ideal for locust breeding. The length of the Takazze river is about 375 miles (600 kilometres).

One of the main aims in walking through parts of the Takazze Valley would have been to verify reports of locust activity. If, indeed, locust swarms traversed the area, possibly breeding along the way, then control measures could be undertaken to reduce as far as possible the size of the escape of the next generation. Also, if swarms of locusts were to 'hold up' for resting purposes in the Takazze area, then a locust control operation could be mounted to kill as many adult locusts as possible before the remnants of the swarms continued to fly southwards. In either, or both, cases this would have a positive impact in terms of protecting vegetation, especially agricultural crops, further south. For example, in some years, locust damage to crops in the Harar and Dire Dawa areas in south–eastern Ethiopia had been so severe that some crops had been totally destroyed. Stemming from this, some people had suffered starvation, while others had hanged themselves on trees, opting for a quicker death.

While studying the geography of the Takazze Valley, inevitably I found myself distracted by the historical reasons for the Takazze's notoriety. It is said that in about 900 BC King Menelik I of Axum, in Northern Ethiopia, made a historic journey. King Menelik claimed he was the offspring of the union between King Solomon and the Queen of Sheba. King Menelik followed the route of the Takazze river on a return journey from Jerusalem to Axum; the Kingdom of Axum was the royal capital where Kings and Queens were crowned. Legend tells that on his return to Ethiopia, King Menelik brought with him the Ark of the Covenant, which contained the stone tablets which were Hebrew-inscribed with the Ten Commandments; the Ten Commandments date from the time of Moses in about 1300 BC. Most Christians in Ethiopia believe that the Ark was housed for perhaps 2,500 years or so in the Axum monastic complex of Our Lady Mary of Zion; they also believe that it was eventually moved to a secret hiding place for safe-keeping. Most churches, as well as houses of Ethiopian Christian believers, have on display a replica of the Ark, which serves as a shrine for prayer.

Reverting now to my planned fact-finding expedition to selected parts of the Takazze Valley, by March of 1955 my plan was complete and final preparations were in progress for my departure. There were some who strongly urged me not to undertake the journey. Although these well-intentioned people recognised the potential benefits of my expedition, at the same time there were reservations about my personal safety. It was known that parts of the Takazze were used to shelter escaped convicts, murderers and brigands. So if I were to undertake my journey and fall into murderous hands, what would become of me? At the age of 24 I felt that the benefit of finding out the true locust situation in the Takazze Valley outweighed possible personal risks. I had already had plenty of first-hand experience of the disastrous impact on human life caused by ravaging locust swarms. In terms of subsistence farming and large-scale agricultural production, too much was at stake to be intimidated by the risk of personal security.

About a week before my departure with carefully chosen Eritrean and Ethiopian colleagues, to my shock and disbelief, I received a message from the director in Nairobi. Apparently, the DLC senior field officer in Somaliland had quarrelled with senior members of the Somali government. As a result, the government had requested that the senior field officer should be replaced. Given the delicate circumstances, I should transfer to take over the duties of the senior field officer within seven days.

So my plan of investigating the locust situation in the Takazze Valley did not come to fruition. Quite suddenly, in the early spring of 1955 I found myself again at the DLC headquarters in Hargeisa, the main town of Somaliland.

Being on familiar ground, it did not take long for me to gain a basic understanding of the locust situation. However, in 1955 there was a change in the weather pattern. In turn, this change was to make a dramatic impact on the overall locust situation.

The climate change involved rain or, to be more precise, lack of it. When I had arrived in Hargeisa, I had noticed that much of the vegetation looked weak and dry. So I checked the rainfall which had been recorded in the previous November and December at a number of weather stations located across Somaliland. The weather picture which emerged was clear: the winter rains had failed. Now, the spring rains should have started; again, this was not the case.

The potentially devastating effects of the dry weather conditions had not been lost on the Protectorate Government. In order to combat possible drought conditions, several relief depots had been established, for instance in Abdel Kadr. These relief stations would provide water and food to those in need.

As far as the usual invasion of locust swarms was concerned, there were many reports of swarms crossing the Somali coast. The total area of the invasion would amount to about 1,000 square miles (2,600 square kilometres). How would the climate change affect the behaviour of the locusts?

The answer to this question soon became apparent. Some of the locust field officers reported that in their areas, locust swarms had arrived and settled in the dry vegetation. In spite of the lack of food for the locusts to devour, the locusts had matured, turning yellow. Breeding then ensued. At this point, because of the lack of rain the female locusts met an insurmountable problem. For the female locust to deposit her egg pod, moist, sandy earth is essential. In large areas, suitable conditions for the deposit of the egg pods did not exist. For a day or so, the females would frantically move from place to place, apparently searching for soft ground. After many vain attempts to lay their eggs, the females would deposit their eggs on the surface of the ground. Soon the eggs would dry in the hot sun – and perish. Sometimes the females flew into trees and high bushes to roost for the night. At dawn, a yellow carpet of eggs would appear on the ground below; the eggs would soon dry and expire.

The implications of this extraordinary situation were obvious. If the spring rains failed, or were patchy, then the progeny of huge swarms would simply die through natural causes, resulting from lack of moist conditions for effective locust egg-laying. If dryness occurred on a large scale, then the locust plague in the Somaliland area would be brought to an end. If this happened, then crops and grazing for livestock in fertile areas to the south, stretching as far as Kenya and Tanzania, would be spared the scourge of the desert locust.

I lost no time in explaining the situation to the field officers, together with a plan of action which would extend to the middle of the year. Normal surveillance of the locust situation would continue. However, in areas where rain had fallen and breeding had progressed, efforts to control the hatching locust hoppers would be redoubled so as to minimise the eventual escape of the next locust generation. If these efforts were successful, then the combination of dried eggs and a limited escape of flying locusts could result in death of the escaping locusts through natural causes; these causes would include attacks by birds, exhaustion caused by strong upper air winds, and so forth.

All went to work to achieve our goal of possibly bringing the locust plague to an end, at least for the year 1955. Throughout the months of April and May, I watched the situation closely. Although rain had fallen in some areas, there was no general rain. So the pattern of female locusts laying their eggs on dry ground continued.

Towards the end of May we received an unexpected report from the mountainous and hilly area around Erigavo in north–eastern Somaliland. This was the first time that a report of locusts harbouring so early in that area had been received. All of the locust field officers were hard at work in their areas, either making reconnaissances or organising locust control measures. I had no wish that any dislocation of the work of the field officers should occur by asking one of them to investigate the Erigavo report. I therefore decided to undertake the task myself.

Three days later I was en route to Erigavo, using two Land Rovers. I was well used to the road surface, which alternated between soft sand and a hard, pot-holed surface. We were heading for Burao, a town I had worked in as a subaltern during my National Service in 1950. As we approached the town, as on previous occasions, we realised we were looking at a mirage. One could see the white buildings of the town seemingly floating on a misty, sponge-like base. As we neared the mirage we could see the large, block-like, white buildings clearly. But as we approached the town, the mirage quickly fragmented – and disappeared. We were faced with another 15 miles of driving before actually reaching Burao.

We continued driving for another two hours past Burao. At last, after a full day's drive of about 250 miles, we made a small camp for the night. Before a good night's rest in my sleeping bag, in the stillness of the desert I watched the heavens for about an hour. As usual, I could clearly see the Great Bear (Ursa Major) and Orion and it was fascinating to watch the shooting stars as each smoothly made its journey through the glittering galaxy.

When I had been asleep for some hours, I was awoken by a strange noise; in the quietude of the night, the noise seemed to be of a gently flowing liquid. Curious in my dry and barren surroundings, I left my camp bed and walked, in the dead of night, toward the strange noise. Soon I could see the silhouette of a Land Rover. And a few seconds later I found one of the drivers sucking a tube, the end of which he quickly placed into a jerrycan which had a capacity of four and a half gallons. The other end had been placed in the petrol tank of the vehicle. I realised instantly that the driver was stealing our petrol; he would sell the petrol privately, as soon as the opportunity arose for him to do so. I asked him for an explanation of what he was doing. He had nothing to say, except that he was sorry and that he realised he would soon have to return to Hargeisa.

Figure 11. Somaliland, 1953. A dry riverbed, or wadi – Somali: toug. *Tougs often served as tracks for motor transport. From time to time, after rain in the hills,* tougs *would flood; the ensuing fast-moving wall of water could be life-threatening.*

By six o'clock in the morning we were again on the dusty, rough road, heading for Erigavo, some 250 miles to the north–east. By midday we were climbing steadily towards the town. When we were about 20 miles from our destination, quite suddenly the sun disappeared behind huge, rolling, dark clouds. Within a few minutes we found ourselves in a deluge of rain accompanied by sheet lightning and loud claps of thunder. Was this the Somaliland of desert, scrub and dust?

We pressed on. But after a few hundred yards we were forced to stop. In front of us was a wadi (which the Somalis call a *toug*) and the *toug* was in flood. Deep sandy-coloured water was roaring down the *toug* with ear-splitting ferocity. The *toug* was about 35 yards wide and a concrete wall, with the width of the road, spanned the *toug* for the use of vehicles. As the water hit the top of the concrete, there was an ear-splitting crash and great, surging waves rose up before our eyes. We were awed by the sheer force of the water. Although we were standing in torrential rain, it was evident that most of the water had originated from the mountains and hills to the north, around Erigavo. Although we had been caught in a heavy storm, we would soon find out that these storms were isolated. This was a heavy shower, rather than part of widespread rain.

After we had waited for about three hours for the water to subside, the Somali supervisor walked to the concrete crossing and waded a few yards into the water. He reported that although the flow of the water remained quite strong, in his judgement we could attempt the crossing in the Land Rovers. We agreed and employed our standard technique. A heavy, strong rope was attached to the rear of the first Land Rover and the other end was latched around the front bumper of the second Land Rover. I told our team that I would drive the first vehicle. If, through the force of the water, the driver of the second vehicle saw that my Land Rover was veering towards the edge of the concrete crossing, then the second vehicle would reverse and pull my Land Rover back on to dry land. If, as we expected, I reached the far side of the crossing, then I would help the second Land Rover by pulling the vehicle through the water.

Using first gear, I steadily drove to the edge of the water; the earlier ferocious torrent had considerably abated. I glanced in the side mirror. The driver behind me was smiling and his arm waved me ahead. As I entered the water I turned the lock against the flow of the water. I progressed steadily. But suddenly, at about the halfway point, there was a surge of the torrent, which hit the door with a loud crack. Within a second I could see rushing water crashing against the window of the door. After another second or two I could see the water forcing its way into the cabin; within a few seconds the seats were awash. Now, in spite of the lock turned to the flow of the water, the vehicle was being steadily pushed towards the edge of the crossing; I had earlier judged the drop from the top of the crossing into the *toug* to be about 15 feet. Now I expected to be dragged out of the utterly hopeless situation.

But nothing happened.

It took just a second or two to face the reality. I was alone. And, inch by inch the vehicle in which I was sitting, was inexorably moving to the edge of the crossing. My first thought was how to escape. I thought that if I could open the door of the Land Rover, then I could clamber onto the hood above. Then, as the vehicle was pushed by the force of the water over the edge of the crossing, I would jump away from the vehicle and try to swim to the bank of the *toug*. The possibility of stones or rocks impeding my escape was a factor beyond my control.

I took hold of the door latch and tried to open the Land Rover door. I pushed the door with all my strength. The door opened slightly, but the force of the water was far stronger than all the strength I could summon. After some water had gushed into the cabin, the door was slammed shut against me. Convinced that my fate was sealed, I simply sat in the water-logged Land Rover – and waited for the inevitable plunge. I could feel the Land Rover continuing its gradual path to the edge. I expected the final push within seconds.

Then I suddenly realised that the Land Rover had stopped moving. Feeling confused, I looked out at the flowing water. Was the torrent subsiding? Yes! I sat in the Land Rover for 20 minutes. Then I tried to open the door; and this time I was successful. I hoisted myself upwards and stood on the frame of the hood. My Somali colleagues were gesticulating and shouting from the edge of the *toug*. I heard nothing except the noise of the rushing water.

Sitting on the frame of the Land Rover hood, I noticed that the rain had stopped and the rays of the sun were beginning to make themselves felt through my saturated clothes. After another 20 minutes I watched one of the Somalis wading into the water; then he bent down. Yes, he had retrieved one end of the broken rope. After he had found the other end, he tied the ends together in a huge knot. Five minutes later my Land Rover found itself on dry land. And an hour later, after the carburettor had been dried and cleaned, we traversed the *toug*; by now the water was ankle-deep and flowing slowly. At last, we were covering the final stretch of our drive to Erigavo.

Erigavo is the main town in the north–east of Somaliland. Situated at about 6,000 feet (1,800 metres) above sea level, the town enjoys a healthy climate of warm days and cool evenings. Erigavo is close to the Somali maritime escarpment which zigzags at various distances from the sea along the northern part of Somaliland. The highest point of the escarpment is a mountain close to Erigavo, which is called Shimbirr. *Shimbirr* in Somali means 'birds'. The mountain rises to 8,400 feet (2,560 metres) above sea level. Upon arrival in Erigavo, I called on the district commissioner; he told me the guest house was reserved for me and he asked that I should meet him in his office early the following morning. The temperature was already dropping, so compared to sleeping in a tent, the cosy guest house was much more comfortable.

I spent two hours in discussion next day with the district commissioner. Like most administrative officers of the British Colonial Service, he proved to be a knowledgeable man on all sorts of matters relating to the Erigavo area. In passing, I should record that I have met, and worked with, a good number of members of the British Administrative Colonial Service; without exception I found these men to be thoroughly competent, dedicated, straightforward and courteous.

So I was not surprised that the district commissioner had a good general knowledge of the locust threat and strongly supported my intended mission to investigate the reports of swarms of breeding locusts. He confirmed that the rains had been patchy, rather than general; he also explained that he had received reports of quite heavy rainfall north–east of Erigavo, in the foothills of the maritime escarpment. If these reports were true, then this area would be ideal for locust breeding. Finally, he told me that the people who lived in the hills were usually cooperative, as long as they understood what was being done, especially if a project was in their best interests. Although occasional hostility had been encountered, he did not expect trouble in our case. Therefore he saw no necessity to offer us an armed escort by members of the police. In any case, he would send word to the Elders of the area that he expected their full cooperation in supporting us in our important work. Due to other pressing assignments, he would not be able to visit us, wherever we might decide to camp; however, in a week or two he would arrange for his deputy to visit and offer us any possible support.

Soon we were once more on the road, this time heading for the escarpment. The first part of the journey was unforgettably beautiful as we drove through dense vegetation of uncountable shades of green. Then we traversed part of a forest of Juniper trees, before descending steeply towards the coastline. We drove eastwards along the sandy coast; although we saw few people, whenever we had the opportunity we asked them if they had heard of, or perhaps seen, locust swarms. Using this word of mouth method, we were led to the area where locusts had been breeding.

As we continued eastwards along the coastal plain, the dryness of the landscape was punctuated by small patches of yellow beneath some of the trees. These patches were, in fact, millions of locust eggs. In that dry landscape, the mature adult locusts could find no soft areas to lay their eggs. Apparently, the locusts could contain the egg pods no longer, so the eggs had been deposited on the surface of the dry ground. Soon they would dry in the hot sun.

As we progressed further east, we noticed that the vegetation became altogether livelier. At one point we stopped to test the sandy loam; it seemed damp and quite soft. Then we were joined by three tribesmen; they told us that they had seen a very large swarm some days previously, which had flown in over the sea. The locusts had rested near the sea, but they did not breed on the plain. The swarm had taken off and flown towards the hills. The tribesmen had heard that the locusts were breeding in the hills. I was a little surprised that the main breeding area was in the foothills of the escarpment, rather than in the sandy areas along the coast. Probably, this was because most rain had fallen inland; so the loam was soft and ideal for the females to lay their eggs.

By nightfall we had established our camp. We would have preferred to camp closer to the hilly area, but the broken terrain, stones and boulders prevented this. Next morning I asked the supervisor to find four locust scouts; these would be men who knew the hills and also had a knowledge of how to identify locust egg fields. The supervisor said he would probably find the right men in a nearby small village called Goureh.

Before fully embarking on the task that lay before us, I decided to make contact with the DLC headquarters in Hargeisa. The field radio was unloaded from a Land Rover and placed on a box in the shade of an *acacia* tree. Sitting in a camp chair, I was soon in contact with my colleagues in the Hargeisa base.

While I was bringing them up to date with a status report, suddenly I heard the noise of a Land Rover engine. Fortunately, I looked behind me. The Land Rover was about 20 yards from me and it was being driven straight at me. The driver was accelerating; now I was looking at the vehicle's radiator. I threw myself to the side and a wheel almost ran over me as it passed and hit the radio with a heavy thud; my transmitter instantly disintegrated and the surrounding sand was littered with pieces of metal. My chair was transformed into wooden fragments.

The vehicle came to a standstill after about 20 yards. The driver got out and approached me. It was the driver whom I had seen stealing our petrol. His expression was sullen. He said he was sorry, that his brakes had failed. I then drove the Land Rover for about 15 minutes; the brakes functioned normally. I suspended the driver from his work. The supervisor explained that there was no risk that the driver might disappear. Being a member of a tribe in the vicinity of Hargeisa, he could never associate with the tribesmen who lived in the area where we were now working. Not only would he be ignored; he knew that in certain circumstances, his life would be at risk.

Within three days we had a good understanding of the size of our task. The area of infestation was about 40 square miles. Within the area there were already pockets of young hoppers (locust nymphs). After two to three weeks, these bands of hoppers would join forces with other bands. Within a day or two, armies of hoppers would be marching through the bush, eating practically all forms of vegetation along the way.

As I had requested on the radio, the bait-laden Dodge Power Wagons soon arrived. After unloading the bait, one of the trucks was sent back to Hargeisa. Its driver carried a letter to the headquarters' administrative officer in which I explained the incident when I had narrowly avoided being hit by the accelerating Land Rover. I also requested a replacement driver – and a replacement field radio! The driver who had committed the offending act was the only passenger in the returning truck.

I judged that we had about five weeks to kill the hoppers before the mature locusts took flight. If the infestation could not be controlled, the escaping locust swarm would probably

Figure 12. Goureh, north–eastern Somaliland, 1955. At the foot of the maritime escarpment; burden camels with locust bait (bran mixed with 1 per cent insecticide). The author stands on the left.

cover more than 200 square miles. Based on my earlier preliminary assessment, I had already requested that three Dodge Power Wagons should be filled with sacks of locust bait and that the convoy should reach us within three days.

We then organised our work. At 2.30 a.m. each morning a train of burden camels laden with locust bait would be led 18 miles to the area of the foothills; the camels were the first to leave because they covered only about two and a half miles per hour. There, the sacks of bait would be transferred to mules. These animals would be led into the hills. Once the hopper-infested area had been reached, the bran bait would be spread before the bands of hoppers. The hoppers would eat the bait and almost instantly die of stomach poisoning.

As the weeks passed, the work progressed well. I accompanied our team on most days. I became used to leaving our camp at 3.30 in the morning and returning by about seven in the evening. I ate a small breakfast; and soup in the evening proved adequately sustaining for what was, after all, quite strenuous exercise. During the day we drank water from a goatskin; and if we found the midday sun to be unbearably hot, we would rest under the umbrella-type boughs of an *acacia* tree.

After about three weeks' work, feeling confident that all was progressing well, I mentioned one day to the supervisor that I would not walk to the hills on the following day. I would have a rest day and possibly reconnoitre the area within a few miles of our camp. At about seven o'clock next day I started walking, alone, to the west of the camp. I was intrigued that the locusts had chosen the foothills for breeding, rather than lay their eggs on the flat area between the sea and the hills. The vegetation at sea level was green, so evidently it had rained along the coast.

At one point I noticed ahead what seemed to be an amorphous heap of dark grey and brown; perhaps they were rags. As I drew closer to the shapeless heap, I realised that the heap was inhabited by a small woman, who apparently was in deep slumber. I thought she was almost certainly ill; perhaps she was suffering from malaria. As far as her belongings were concerned she had none, although a small, dirty-looking kettle rested near her head; the kettle was without a lid and a little water glistened slightly in the sunshine.

I knelt down beside the motionless woman and gently felt her forehead. Within a second the woman opened her eyes. With a shocked shriek, she raised her head, took hold of the handle of the kettle and hugged it in her bosom. Glaring at me, suddenly she swung the kettle as fast as she was able; the swing came to an abrupt end as the kettle hit my head. Astonished at her reaction, and with a wet head, I withdrew and continued my walk.

This was a woman who typified the low end of the spectrum of wealth in our world. Many of us have the privilege of living in a so-called developed part of the world, where human beings can, and do, amass seemingly endless wealth. And then we have the vast, less-developed part of the world, where millions of human beings live in wretched, abject poverty, like that woman. She carried with her what was, for her, a very valuable piece of property; this was her dirty kettle. It could well have been her only property; and she was afraid I wanted to steal her possession!

The image of this woman, who lived in absolute poverty, will remain imprinted forever in my remembrance. For me, this woman continues to symbolise the lot of millions of human beings, most of whom live in the Third World.

After walking for about two hours, I had not seen a single locust. The sun was becoming hot, so I thought of returning to our camp. I walked a little further; after a short distance I found myself looking into a *toug*. My eyes followed the course of the *toug* towards the mountain escarpment; turning towards the sea, this wide channel descended to the seashore. The sea, which was the Gulf of Aden, was washing gently to the shore; as I looked towards the horizon, I was struck by the sparkling surface of this vast stretch of water, which reflected the rays of the sun streaming down from an azure sky. At the point where I was standing, the *toug's* walls were 35–40 feet deep; and the floor of the *toug* was about 40 yards wide. I wondered how many thousands of years had passed since the first rivulet snaked its way to the sea. And over the following years, the rushing waters from the mountains had carved its ever deeper course.

I walked a few hundred yards towards the sea; now the walls were far less deep. I scrambled down to the floor of the *toug*, crossed the floor and scrambled up the other side. With the heat of the sun beating down I would soon turn back, perhaps following a return direction a little more inland. Ahead of me was a bank of green bushes which were growing in a shallow depression. Evidently the rain had extended to this area; and perhaps I might find some locusts there.

When I was about 40 yards from the bushes ahead, I suddenly heard wild shouts. I was startled and at the same time mystified. Suddenly about 15 men appeared from the bushes; and they were running towards me. My reactions were a little slow. Instead of taking immediate flight, I stood there for a second or so simply wondering what was happening. Then I saw two or three large stones flying towards me. I turned and ran.

Now stones were landing all around me; each hit the ground with a thud. I could clearly hear the voices of my pursuers; and since I had learned the Somali language, the incessant loud shouting pierced the still air: 'Kill him! Kill him!' Were they gaining ground on me? After about 300 yards, I realised I was nearing the edge of the *toug*. I looked back. The howling mob was now smaller, but six or seven men were still running towards me. I had little time to decide whether I should let myself fall against the wall of the *toug*. I turned to look over the edge. At that moment, a stone hit my right ear. Momentarily, a thought flashed through my mind – where would I be if the stone had hit my head two inches to the left?

Now I was sliding down the wall of the *toug*. I tried to aim for protruding parts of the wall, hoping that my fall might be slowed. In a few seconds I landed at the bottom of the wall, 35 feet or so below. Shaken, I picked myself up and ran obliquely across the floor of the *toug*, towards the sea. I could still hear the shouting of my pursuers and I could hear stones thudding behind me. I looked back. About six of the men were shouting abuse at me from the top of the wall of the *toug*. With difficulty, I clambered up the opposite wall, which was now somewhat lower. I told myself to be grateful that I was still in one piece. I was sweating profusely and drops of sweat blurred my vision.

I walked as quickly as I could back to the camp. I found myself wondering where the attackers had come from. Certainly, it was an organised attack. So as I had earlier walked alone on the coastal plain, had these men been shadowing me before crouching behind the bushes in the depression? And were they shadowing me now? I tried to quicken my step, but in vain.

Panting and saturated with sweat, at last I reached our camp. It was only then that I realised I had sprained my ankle, which was rapidly swelling. A few hours later the supervisor entered my tent; he had arrived about three hours earlier than expected. He explained that word of the attack on me had reached him while at work in the hills, so he had returned to camp without delay.

When nearing our camp he had stopped for some tea at a small village. He had heard the Elders talking in quiet, low tones to one another; they were almost whispering. The Elders agreed that our presence in their area was unnecessary. They considered it important that I should be dealt with. They then agreed that I should be murdered during the darkness of the coming night.

The supervisor told me that to give me this news saddened him. He felt that we had no time to lose and that we should dismantle the camp and leave. I pointed out that we had a responsibility to see our work finished; a way must be found to achieve this. I asked him to give some thought to this and we should meet again in about a half hour. In the meantime, some preparations could be made for our departure, in the early evening.

About 15 minutes later we heard the sound of an approaching vehicle. As I hobbled out of the tent, a Land Rover came into view. A man of about 27 years of age got out and cheerfully shook my hand. 'Ah, yes,' he said with a courteous smile, 'You must be Colin Everard. I am the deputy to the district commissioner; he said I should find you and see how things are progressing. I hope all is well?' This was a pleasant man and he often smiled happily. But when I told him the story of the day, his expression altogether changed. He summoned three armed policemen who accompanied him.

Within minutes they had left with our supervisor under instructions to arrest the Elders on a charge of attempted murder.

Next morning, the deputy DC had the men brought before him. Their faces betrayed forlorn bewilderment; perhaps this was, I thought, because a totally unforeseen fate had overtaken them. Through an interpreter, the deputy DC explained that in his role of representing the government, he was an authorised magistrate. He asked me to recount my experience of the previous day, which I did. He then heard evidence from the supervisor. Finally, he asked first myself, and then the supervisor, whether we could recognise any of those who had attacked me, or had conspired to have me murdered. I recognised one man, the supervisor two.

Before passing judgement, the deputy asked each man in turn whether he wished to make a statement. Again, one noticed the look of dismay and hopelessness on the faces of the accused. The response of each was similar, namely the men admitted their guilt and now realised they were mistaken in their actions, which they regretted. Two of the men expressed incredulity that the deputy DC had arrived at the scene at the critical moment. Might this be the hand of Allah? The deputy DC then sentenced the men to terms of imprisonment. He said a police van would transport them to the prison the following day. Meanwhile, they would be held under police guard. Before the proceedings terminated the deputy issued a stern warning that our work would continue; if any further interference might be reported, the government would react with severity against those who were causing a disturbance of the peace.

Although I had played a part in the proceedings, I did not feel connected to them. Rather, I found myself looking at a somewhat incongruous scene. Where else in the world might one find a court of law established in a remote, isolated area of a tropical land, in the shade of an *acacia* tree?

Of course, rough justice had been meted on the Elders. On the other hand, the Elders had admitted their guilt, so in basic terms, the punishment given was justified. And one should not ignore the fact that my colleagues and I were simply doing our job. In such circumstances, should our lives be put at risk?

Before leaving us, the deputy DC told me that two armed policemen would remain with us until our work was finished. He expected their presence to act as a deterrent against possible violence. Thanking him for his timely intervention, we bade the deputy DC *adieu*. I told him we expected our work to be finished in about two to three weeks.

The work continued, although for the following two weeks I remained in the camp while my ankle healed. After almost three weeks, the systematic locust control campaign came to an end. By this time my ankle had healed, so I was able to participate in the final check of the locust-infested area. This took two full days. To avoid walking twice between our camp and the hills, we slept overnight in the hilly area. At the end of the second day, we were satisfied that our control efforts had been successful.

Now it was time to leave, which we did. In Erigavo, I briefed the district commissioner on what we had been doing; he invited me to a delightful lunch. Now again, we were travelling, this time with Hargeisa as our destination. There, I studied all reports received from the locust control officers. Somaliland was effectively free of locusts. The escape from various breeding areas had been minimal; so this would mean that agricultural crops and grazing further south had been saved from potential destruction by ravenous locust swarms. In turn hunger, even starvation, on a large scale had been prevented. Our objective had been achieved.

6

The Tip of the Horn of Africa

In 1957, I was appointed as the liaison officer between the Desert Locust Control (DLC), the headquarters of which was based in Nairobi in Kenya, and the Locust Department of the UN Italian Trusteeship of Somalia. Control of locust infestations was crucial in the context of preventing large-scale locust invasions of agricultural areas in the south of Somalia and in Kenya; however, the financial infrastructural resources needed to combat large-scale locust infestations in Somalia were too limited to mount effective widespread anti-locust campaigns.

In order to overcome the dilemma, an agreement had been reached that when the Somalia budget for locust operations became exhausted, the government could make a request for supplementary funding to the DLC liaison officer in Mogadishu. This was far from a 'rubber stamp' procedure; an instalment of additional funding was provided only after a thorough, although diplomatically courteous, investigation had been made by the liaison officer to ensure that the request was properly supported by the actual situation. And sometimes a positive response by the liaison officer was delayed or refused due to malpractices of Somali officials. Delicate discussions might even be called for at ministerial level, before what was irregular had been effectively righted. At all times, I was conscious of the fact that we were dealing with other people's money – usually that of the East African taxpayer.

The Liaison Officer of the DLC was its only member to be based in Mogadishu, the capital city of Somalia. Within three years, Mogadishu would become the capital of the Somali Republic, a country which would embrace Somaliland to the north. As a centre of trade, Mogadishu had existed for about 1,000 years. After visits by Greek vessels in ancient times, its development had been greatly influenced by Arab countries to the north. In fact, over the centuries the Somali coastal area, including Mogadishu, was ruled by a series of sultans.

In the nineteenth century the Italians arrived as colonisers. As a part of Italian East Africa, heavy investment was made in the transportation system, as well as in agriculture. The flagship tar-bound macadam road project was the Strada Imperiale; this was a road planned and constructed, mainly using Italian labour, to link Mogadishu with Addis Ababa in Ethiopia. When completed, the road would cover a distance of some 620-odd miles (1,000 kilometres). As far as agricultural development was concerned, much investment was made in banana production, especially along the banks of the two large rivers which flow through the southern part of Somalia; these rivers are called the Shebelle or *Webi Schiabelli*, which means Leopard River, and the Juba.

At the time of my arrival in Mogadishu, it was a small city which functioned well. Apart from Arab-type buildings there were a number of older buildings which, typically, were supported by imposing, heavily built, weathered walls. And especially in the centre of the city, there were a good number of white buildings which had been erected during the era of Italian colonisation. So the appearance of the centre of the city was of unmatching buildings which reflected both Arabian and Italian cultural influences, a mixture of styles rather pleasing to the eye. Inland, behind the city, the ground rose towards a long ridge. Standing on the ridge, one could admire the white and darker coloured buildings which bordered the vastness of the Indian Ocean, normally a calm sea which seemed to stretch forever to the horizon.

During my tenure as liaison officer, the management of the Somali anti-locust organisation soon learned that, provided all was in order, they could rely on my solid support. But if malpractices came to light, then my attitude would quickly change. After some initial misunderstandings, the working relationship between myself and the Somali locust control management developed well, and we soon worked together healthily as a team. Practically all the senior officials were Somali. With approaching independence, few Italian staff remained; those who did, occupied non-executive positions. Although, politically speaking, we found ourselves in a transition phase, each of those involved worked up to the limit of his or her capacity to locate and destroy the common enemy: the desert locust.

Although ostensibly there were stipulated working hours, in fact the norm was that one should be ready to react to the locust invasion situation at any time. Normally, work began at seven o'clock in the morning by participation in the radio network, chaired by the DLC Director in Nairobi. The network stretched from Nairobi to Jeddah in Saudi Arabia, Addis Ababa and Dire Dawa in Ethiopia, Hargeisa in Somaliland and Mogadishu in Somalia. At two o'clock in the afternoon, it was time for lunch and, for some, a siesta in the heat of the day. Work resumed at five o'clock and continued until half past seven in the evening.

With the approaching end of the UN Italian Trusteeship, evening work sessions were often accompanied by the noise of mass political rallies. The main spokesmen who addressed these loud, emotional rallies were Egyptian schoolteachers who had been provided under an aid agreement. The Wind of Change was blowing across Africa. From a cultural viewpoint,

Somalis are characteristically a calm, unaffected people; many have a delightful sense of humour. Now they were being exhorted to hate the foreign imperialists and do away with them as quickly as possible, one way or another. *En passant*, I would mention that, in spite of the frenzied attempts to stir up hate against foreigners (often by those who were, themselves, foreign to the Somali political landscape!), at all times my personal relationships with Somalis remained friendly and down-to-earth, based on mutual respect.

Although the liaison officer worked alone, I was certainly never lonely. Often I found myself doing the rounds; apart from informing myself on the locust situation in Somalia and adjacent countries, I was often asked for advice by the Somali locust control personnel on where and when ground reconnaissances should be planned. In the wider context, diplomatic representatives often invited me to bring them up to date on the general locust situation, as well as the latest techniques being used to combat locust invasions.

Contact with diplomatic representatives regularly extended into the evening hours. Although the Desert Locust Control liaison officer was accorded only basic diplomatic privileges, in fact the diplomatic community in Mogadishu regarded the liaison officer as someone with diplomatic status. In consequence, apart from his sometimes consultative role, the liaison officer was regularly invited, with his wife, to diplomatic receptions. Conversations at these receptions could often be used by the liaison officer to initiate a discussion concerning the need for donor support for the Somali *Anti Acridica* (anti locust) effort.

To attend these receptions was usually a delight, not least due to the often exotic ambiance linked with the ever-present tropical temperature. And the attendance reflected so many cultural variations. Apart from those who wore Somali national dress, silk saris from the subcontinent of India and Pakistan often provided the onlooker with strong splashes of beautiful colour. Or again, the Yemeni ambassador, who would be dressed in white and gold national costume, hand on his long, ornate *jembiya* (dagger), was indeed striking to the eye.

Although the Italian Trusteeship of Somalia was barely touched by the effects of the then Cold War, which had developed between the then Union of Soviet Socialist Republics (USSR) and the West, ugly symptoms of the enmity which existed between the USSR and the West occasionally surfaced during diplomatic receptions. In a general sense, one could say that, at the diplomatic level, there was a consciousness of the Cold War; and because of this there was a tendency at diplomatic parties to look, in particular, for the Russian and American ambassadors and to take note where each was standing in relation to the other. One hoped the two would not be in close proximity; there was always the risk that the combatants might resort to verbal (hopefully diplomatic) sparring.

It was at one of these receptions that, after having been warmly welcomed, my wife and I circulated amongst the assembled throng. Here and there we paused for a short chat with one of our many acquaintances. As we were slowly moving through the guests, we heard some loud voices above the discreet diplomatic chit-chat. Suddenly, there was a hushed, embarrassed silence – except for the vociferous quarrel which had developed between the rival ambassadors of the United States and the USSR. The guests were witnessing the increasing tempo of the adversaries' exchanges. The harsh voices were growing louder by the second; and one sensed that the limit of vocal sparring would inevitably soon be superseded by a gloves-off row. Now, we realised that we were looking at two diplomatic representatives who were involved in a thoroughly undiplomatic situation!

As a neutral, apolitical guest, I strode to the source of the noise. The Russian ambassador was a thick-set, burly man with dark hair which covered his brow; his face was pink, apparently with vexation. The American, a tall, somewhat elderly, distinguished career diplomat, was tensely 'nailing' his adversary by making short, contentious, vocal jabs; the expression on his face was one of grim determination.

'Excellencies,' I interjected in a firm voice, 'It is really a pleasure to see you again. I am sorry to interrupt you, but it is important to bring you up to date with the present desert locust situation in Somalia.' Their Excellencies, taken off balance, turned to me, each seemingly mystified by the abrupt intrusion. Silence ensued. I then spoke to both of them for a few minutes, outlining the current desert locust situation. Just before finishing, I was happy to see another guest button-hole the American ambassador; after a few moments the distracted ambassador was led away. I shook hands with the Russian ambassador and bade him *adieu*. The reception resumed with the buzz of gentle conversation.

A few weeks later, my wife and I received an invitation to attend a reception at the American embassy, which we happily accepted. On arrival, we approached the ambassador who was standing with his wife at the imposing embassy entrance. When he saw me his strong, somewhat craggy face lit up; now he was smiling.

'Good evening, ambassador,' I said.

The ambassador offered me his hand. With a look of the benevolence of an older man, he drew me slightly towards him; then he placed his hand on my shoulder and said in a firm voice, 'Good evening, saviour!'

With hindsight, by 1957 we were well past the midpoint of research and information-gathering which would lead to the development of techniques that would ultimately control locust infestations. For example, research with spraying techniques at ground level had resulted in vehicles being fitted with a drum of insecticide from which a spray was pumped using the force of the vehicle's exhaust. In developing spraying techniques, whether on the ground or in the air, the challenge centred on the need to be able to control the size, dosage and concentration of the spray droplets. The primary aim was to make sure that the droplet size would never lead to excessive spray concentrations, because these could endanger animal and plant life. On the other hand, if the spray droplets were too small, then the spray would diffuse into the atmosphere, the droplets sometimes, in fact, moving upwards instead of downwards towards the locusts. By 1957 it was already evident that the use of vehicles fitted with insecticide spraying gear would, in a good number of locust-infested areas, replace the manual labour used to spread locust bait.

One of the more intriguing, and rewarding, aspects of working in the DLC was the close cooperation which developed between the DLC and the Desert Locust Survey – the DLS. The DLS was the scientific arm of the anti-locust effort. In the 1950s, much of the scientific work undertaken was related to the ground-breaking experimental work undertaken by Sir Boris Uvarov, the brilliant Russian scientist, in the 1920s.

The reality of the situation in the 1950s was that, whether one was a scientist or a layman, potentially all could contribute something to completing the picture of locust behaviour, migratory routes, optimal breeding conditions and so on. The channelling of new knowledge was a one-way process. The locust control man could feed knowledge into the scientific system, where it was received with appreciation. The reverse did not happen, except where experimental control techniques needed to be tested. In a nutshell, all those involved with trying to combat the locust scourge could potentially contribute to knowledge which, when complete, would lead to the ultimate solution in terms of controlling desert locust plagues.

Whether involved directly in locust control measures, back-up administration work or information-gathering,

I found myself with a significant advantage, which sometimes led to an enhancement of the quality of my work. I had learned to speak fluent Somali, a language considered by some to be impossibly complicated from both structural and pronunciation aspects. To some extent, the language was tonal. For example, I recall one word which had three distinct meanings, depending whether the voice was pitched high, medium or low. Such intricacies presented little problem to me.

Because of the reputation of the language as being extremely difficult, usually impossible, for the European ear, I had made no conscious effort to learn the language. However, after spending seven months in 1953 as the only European working with four Somalis, I began to dream in Somali. The next stage began when I realised I was understanding conversations and stories which Somalis related, especially on long journeys. The final stage was reached shortly after, when I heard myself speaking Somali, albeit initially in short phrases. Although I felt this to be a natural development, the reaction of the Somali team was, initially at least, one of stunned amazement.

To speak and understand a language properly, one has to 'hear', and to think in, the foreign language. Languages have idiosyncrasies; the Somali language is no exception. In conversation, the language employs what I would term 'the confirmation negative'. As an example, a desert locust scout meets another locust scout. One says to the other, 'So you didn't see a single locust today, did you?' The response, 'Yes'. (The 'Yes' confirms that the scout did not see a locust.)

In fact, my knowledge of the language was not comprehensive; as with any foreign language one discovered gaps in my vocabulary. However, the level of my Somali language knowledge, linked with perfect pronunciation and intonation, was more than adequate for my work, whether at the functional or diplomatic levels. Because of the degree of my knowledge of the language, most Somalis thought that I had a complete mastery of their language, which was not, in fact, the case.

While in Mogadishu, Somali senior officials were sometimes intrigued that a European could talk to them not only in their own language, but with what they described as 'pure' expression. They stated that this was in contrast to the type of Somali they themselves spoke, which contained Arabic, Italian and even Swahili vocabulary. The explanation for this contrast was that, by chance, I had learned the language in the interior, whereas the Somali spoken along the coastal area was influenced by speakers of other languages, especially Arabic.

By 1957 I felt that I had gained a good deal of hands-on experience, at least in north–eastern Africa, in the field of locust control. I had worked in both Ethiopia and Eritrea, as well as in Somaliland. Now I had the opportunity to broaden my experience in the UN Trusteeship of Somalia.

One of the practical problems which confronted the locust field officer was the requirement to obtain a visa when, for example, one needed to cross the border between Somalia and Ethiopia. Locust swarms are very mobile; our field officers needed to be equally mobile. Locusts did not recognise borders; but our field officers needed to apply for and obtain a visa before they could cross the border. Delays inevitably ensued.

I felt that if I could persuade the Somali government to relax and speed up the visa procedure, then perhaps we could convince the Ethiopian government of the benefit of making a reciprocal arrangement.

I therefore requested a meeting with the Somali Interior Minister. On the appointed day, I was courteously received by the handsome Minister; his office was on the second floor of a substantial government building. The Minister looked to be in good shape physically; he struck me as a man in his late 30s. Instead of wearing Somali dress, he wore a well-cut, dark suit. He sat behind a large desk in his spacious office; from time to time, the Minister turned his head and seemed to stare through a floor-to-ceiling window. He was, in fact, looking at the sea, which was the Indian Ocean.

After courteous exchanges, I began to explain the visa problem. I requested consideration of a procedural mechanism under which designated DLC field officers could be granted multi-entry visas with a validity of, say, one year.

While I was talking, I heard loud voices outside the Minister's door. With staccato shrieks and longer cries, the noise seemed to be increasing. Now there was banging on the door.

The Minister interrupted me. 'Mr Everard. I do apologise for the noise on the landing. You see, we feel our citizens must have their democratic rights. Each of those noisy people are asking for help. Of course, they won't get anything from the government. But they are allowed to ask.' He smiled briefly.

Suddenly, the office door burst open. About 12 people rushed towards the Minister's desk. For a moment, the Minister looked alarmed. Then he saw four armed policemen enter his office, led by a sergeant. The Minister nodded to the sergeant. Immediately, the intruders were beaten about their heads and bodies. The mob was hounded from the office. Three of the intruders were lying, semi-conscious and groaning, on the floor. The policemen dragged them from the office.

Now all was quiet. The Minister turned his head to look at the calm sea. Then he turned his head and looked at me once more. 'You were saying, Mr Everard?'

The meeting ended soon afterwards. I followed up our meeting with a confirmation letter. In spite of a reminder, I received no response.

Once my duties as the liaison officer were progressing on an even keel, I felt free to look ahead for what I hoped would be useful challenges. And looking at the overall locust picture at that time, I asked myself whether our knowledge concerning locust behaviour was adequate, or whether there were further unanswered questions.

This led me to identify what I thought might be an important question relating to locust migratory routes. Detailed knowledge of migratory routes was of crucial importance in the context of positioning our field personnel in the right areas and in good time to prepare and undertake locust control campaigns.

As far as locust invasions of the northern part of the Somali peninsula were concerned, locust swarms typically arrived from the north and north–west during August and September. The extent of these swarms covered about 1,000 square miles. Although little was known about where the locusts rested before flying south from mid-October onwards, there was an assumption that the locusts held up in the hills and mountains which straddle, from east to west, the northern Somali area. It was assumed that the swarms remained in the mountains until they moved southwards to breed; one sometimes heard a reference that swarms were harboured in the Erigavo hills in the north–east of Somaliland. However, because we received few reports of locust swarms in the mountainous area during the late summer months, I questioned this assumption. Could it be, for example, that the swarms moved further east towards the tip of the Horn of Africa? If they could be found there, then they could be controlled *in situ*. This action would greatly diminish the escaping swarms which would fly to the south to breed, once the north–east monsoon established itself several weeks later.

With this in mind I asked for a meeting with senior members of the Somalia Locust Control organisation. After explaining what I thought we needed to know, I asked whether the Somalis had made a locust information-gathering reconnaissance in the far north of the country.

My question was met with silence. The blank expressions on the faces of my colleagues gave me the answer. Then the senior of the group, Ali Nur, spoke.

'Colin, no, we haven't been up there and we don't know much about the area. We certainly have no idea whether locust swarms invade the area. You have to understand that we are mostly from tribes who live in the lower half of the country. So I don't think we would be welcomed up there; after all we are talking about an area which is at least 1,500 kilometres to the north of here. If we were to travel up there, who knows, we could be killed!'

'Thank you,' I responded. 'I think this is an important subject. After all, if we find out that swarms congregate somewhere near Cape Guardafui, which is the tip of the Horn of Africa, then we could carry out control measures and perhaps hit the generation of adults so hard that control of the next generation further south would be much easier. I will plan to make a trip up there from mid-May. Fortunately, as a European, I don't have to think about other tribes.'

Preparations for my trip were routine. I was used to reconnaissance work throughout the Horn of Africa. In this case, however, there was an intriguing difference, in the sense that I would be travelling to a remote area which, up to that point, had not been reconnoitred by locust control personnel.

The day before leaving with two Land Rovers for the first stage of the journey, I was working on last-minute tasks in my office. There was a tap on the door. It was Ali Nur. He said simply,

'Colin, I understand you are leaving tomorrow. You know, you may be in for a few surprises up there in the north; who knows – only Allah! We don't like the idea of you going up there with just a helper. I would like to come with you.'

The following day we left for Belet Uen and I was happy to have Ali Nur with me as a good colleague who, in time, would become a solid friend. A particular advantage in having him with us was that he knew a number of locust control assistants who, on a day-to-day basis, worked from towns and villages; their main task was to keep their area under surveillance and report on locust movements. However, there were no assistants in the extreme north of the country. Apparently, for an unexplained reason, the Somali Locust Control organisation excluded the extreme north from their sphere of work.

The road to Belet Uen was of tarmac, having been constructed by the Italian colonisers; they used mainly Italian labourers for the construction. The journey was pleasant as it followed the course of the Shebelle river. For much of the journey, the road passed through impressive banana plantations. We camped about an hour's drive beyond Belet Uen. Now, instead of driving further west, we took a road which would lead to Galcaio, to the north.

In this part of the world, one normally hoped to cover about 200 miles (320 kilometres) each day. This would be a good average. Faster vehicular travel on dirt roads was the exception; sometimes, roads had become pot-holed to such an extent that a top speed of 10 mph could hardly be reached. Rain damage could also present a problem. In the Horn area there are usually two annual rainy periods; otherwise the country receives no rainfall. When the rains come, intense storms may occur. So the road traveller should never be surprised to suddenly find that stretches of a road have been virtually washed away. There were other hazards, for example small bridges which had been damaged by the elements, which would confront the patient driver and which would need to be overcome. This situation was accepted as part of the everyday working life of the locust officer.

Now we were en route to Galcaio, a provincial town which was situated in central Somalia. For 100 or more miles to the south and north of Galcaio, one drives across a vast gypsum plain. The Land Rover is continuously battered with bumps and vibrations as one traverses the gypsum rock. Tons of gypsum dust belch behind the Land Rover causing a dense cloud. Some of the dust is forced upwards, so that it is not long before the driver and passengers feel a grittiness on their tongues. From time to time, our Somali driver would spit out of the window.

Although we had intended making a camp for the night near Galcaio, I suggested we should press on further north towards Gardo. I hoped we would leave the gypsum behind, which we did, to my relief. I had previously spent some seven months working from Las Anod, in Somaliland to the west of Galcaio, an area also situated on gypsum. I soon learned the local water was brackish, so a short drink had the same effect on the stomach as salts! Working from Las Anod, in order to replenish our supply of drinking water, we travelled 50 miles to the north, to Hudin. There we approached a cave in an outcrop of rocks. Having frightened away a colony of baboons, we removed a boulder and entered the cave. Crawling along a low natural tunnel, after about 25 yards we came to a deep pool of fresh water. From this fresh water source, we could replenish our galvanised water drums.

In any case, the brackish water had made an indelible mark on my memory because of its explosive effect on the stomach. This memory is what persuaded me that we would be better to continue driving until twilight; and even a little beyond. The gypsum terrain had gradually given way to sandy, broken country and the low bushes and small plants reflected the change in the terrain. I asked the driver to stop when he could see an *acacia* tree not far from the narrow dirt road. We carried on; with the short twilight which is normal in countries not far from the equator, the light seemed to be dwindling. Then I saw the driver switch on his headlights. Suddenly he stopped. Before I could speak, the driver opened his door and crouched by the wing of the Land Rover. Now in the headlamps I could see a gazelle; it was walking straight towards the front of the vehicle, seemingly in a daze; it was dazzled by the glare of the lights. Then I saw the driver's hand grab a leg of the animal.

'*Bis-mily-raham-rahim!*' Five seconds later the animal was dead; its throat had been slit by the driver's knife.

That evening, in our little camp under a green umbrella *acacia* tree, the Somalis had a feast and recounted stories to one another until midnight. And I was served a steak dinner by the cook and general helper, who was travelling with us.

Next morning we awoke later than usual. At about six o'clock, as I slipped out of my bed from under the mosquito net, I saw that we had company. Five or six young bushmen were standing in a semi-circle around our camp. Each was dressed in a loin cloth and simple leather sandals; their torsos were gleaming in the tentative rays of the rising sun. Each carried a massive, dense head of crinkly hair. All looked impressively strong. Each of these fine-looking men held a spear at his side.

I pulled on my shorts and approached the group. They made no gesture. I held out my hand.

'Peace. Do we have peace?' I asked in Somali. The men looked at me without movement nor gesture.

I continued, 'I am speaking to you in your own Somali language. Listen. Do we have peace? '

The look on each face became more intense. For about ten seconds these men fixed me with a steady stare. Suddenly, one man let out a shrill cry. Now all were singing in unison. Then they danced in a circle. Finally, each approached me, smiling, and took my hand, exclaiming, 'Peace!'

Once we had explained our mission, each of our visitors became relaxed and friendly; their curiosity had been satisfied. The men related where and when they had seen locusts over the last year or two. While we were talking, two of the men ran off. They rejoined us a half hour later carrying

Figure 13. North of Gardo, Somalia, 1953. A Somali tribesman. He is carrying a headrest on his spear. Somali foot travellers could often give useful information about desert locust swarms or hopper infestations, as well as details of rainfall and prevailing winds.

a wooden pot, which was full of camel's milk; nowadays the milk of a camel is recognised as being highly nutritious. After two hours of questioning and counter-questioning, we were once again en route northwards, towards Gardo.

The vast gypsum plain was well behind us and now we were traversing mostly sandy country which, typically, would be ideal for locust breeding. Apparently, there had been rainfall because the bushes were green and, here and there, we could see ephemeral growth. Sometimes we stopped and spent an hour or so looking for locusts. In fact, we usually found a few, although they were solitary and showed no signs of swarming.

As we progressed northwards, I was struck by the contrast between the relatively pleasant semidesert conditions through which we were driving now, and the changed scene which would confront the traveller in the period of the second half of June to October. It is during this period that the summer wind, the *kharif*, blows.

Here, as a digression, I would like to describe the nature of the contrasting conditions which I have mentioned and which have as their focal point the *kharif* summer wind. I believe that any text on the Horn of Africa would be incomplete without a description of the *kharif*, because this ferocious wind impacts on the everyday lives of most Somalis, especially those who live out their lives in the vast areas of desert or semidesert. I am offering my description of the *kharif* by means of a personal anecdote, which now follows.

Four years previously, as a DLC field officer, I had been based for seven months close to a town in eastern Somaliland called Las Anod. In July 1953 I had arranged (by radio) to meet the DLC's Liaison Officer to the then UN Trusteeship of Somalia; we were to meet a little to the south of Gardo. The Liaison Officer's name was Baxter; he circulated a message that he intended to carry out a desert locust reconnaissance from Mogadishu, as far north as Gardo.

After our meeting and an exchange of information, we bade one another farewell. Baxter started his return journey to the south. As for myself, instead of returning directly westwards on the road to Las Anod, I decided to follow a loop to the north, which would eventually turn south-westwards, in the direction of Las Anod.

Having left at six-thirty in the morning, as intended we drove in a northerly direction; three hours later, we noticed a camel track which seemed to follow a westerly course. So we turned onto it. As we made steady progress, we noticed that the environmental conditions were changing.

The stillness of the dawn had been replaced by a gusting wind. And as the heat of the day increased, so had the strength of the wind; now, agitated patches of sand were swirling around us. By noon, vast clouds of sand were drifting across the landscape, driven by the howling wind, and every so often our vision was briefly blocked by millions of particles of blowing sand.

Yes, the *kharif* wind was now well into its daily task of shifting countless tons of sand to another part of the seemingly limitless semidesert. The source of this yearly phenomenon is off the coast of East Africa, somewhat south of the equator. In its initial stage the wind blows from the south-east. However, as it moves northwards across East Africa the wind turns, until it blows from the south-west. Once in desert or semidesert conditions to the north, the *kharif* gathers force; it blows over Somalia and becomes part of the great sweep of the southwest monsoon flow that reaches southern Asia. The hot, often gale-force wind starts at dawn and continues during the day; the *kharif* blows from the second half of June to October, at which point the north-eastern monsoon gradually prevails.

I had grown used to the *kharif* in Las Anod; however, the town is situated in a vast gypsum plain. So although gypsum dust noisily swirled around our camp, its power and density was Lilliputian compared with the billowing clouds of sand which now cast a huge, dark shroud over us and our surroundings. As the driver did his best to persevere in keeping the Land Rover on the camel track, we were inevitably becoming aware that we might soon lose our way.

Now the visibility was drastically reduced. At about midday we found ourselves in a sunless, murky gloom. Outside the wind was howling and we were enveloped in blowing sand. We became conscious of sand particles which were being forced into our vehicle; and with sand in one's mouth, one talks little and one purses one's lips!

The driver turned to me. 'I am sorry, Mr Everard, we have lost our way. I lost the track a few minutes ago; then I thought I had found it again. But it's gone. Sorry!' His face reflected his helplessness – and his hopelessness.

Rummaging in the few belongings I had brought for an overnight's rest near Gardo, my hand soon felt the case of my compass. I set the compass at a little west of south and I asked the driver to drive over the semidesert on the set course. After about two hours' driving in the gloom, vague forms appeared ahead of us. To our surprise we found ourselves among a cluster of *gurghis*. Then our eyes made out the form of what was almost certainly the only permanent building in what seemed to be a very small village; the single story concrete building may well have been a police post. Seeing no human movement, I concluded that, in those terrible conditions, the village was uninhabited; until the driver stopped in front of a *gurghi*.

An elderly, bearded man appeared, stooping under the small entrance to the *gurghi*. From head to foot he was clad in a toga-like robe which had doubtless been white; now it was strongly tinged with the colour of sand. As he took a step outside, he was joined by two elderly men.

The three of them looked weary. 'Peace,' I said.

The three responded in unison, 'It is peace.' With a look of curiosity, they simply stared at me, unsmiling.

I tried to talk above the howling wind. 'Why do you live here, I mean with the wind and sand?'

'We cannot hear you!' was the response of one. 'The wind is loud. You must shout!'

So I shouted, 'Why do you live here?'

The reply was concisely to the point. 'We live here because this is our *home*!'

The eldest of the three smiled for an instant. Then he led the way back into the *gurghi*. The men had disappeared. So we moved on.

Figure 14. Northern Somalia, October 1957. The effect of the strong south–west wind called the kharif. *Between the months of July and October each year, the* kharif *wind blows countless tons of sand across the Horn of Africa, and beyond. The picture shows a building almost buried in sand; only small parts of the roof remain visible.*

We continued our drive southwards in the gloom with sand swirling around us. After another half hour or so, we sensed that, instead of the smooth sand beneath us, the vehicle vibrated from time to time, as if on an altogether rougher surface. Now the vibrations became more frequent; within another half hour they were virtually continuous. Suddenly, we were in harsh sunlight; and the stark, strongly reflected light grey of gypsum rock struck our eyes. We had crossed the edge of a gypsum rock plain; and our destination, Las Anod, was situated on a gypsum plain!

I asked the driver to stop for a minute; perhaps we might find our bearings on that vast plain. The area for which I had responsibility for locust surveillance stretched over 10,000 square miles. I had already made several reconnaissances, so in the event that there might be some sort of landmark, I felt confident that I might be able to recognise it. The driver pointed to the north–west; then he cupped his hands around his eyes. After a few seconds he told me that in the distance he had seen a moving black object; perhaps he had seen a truck and if this was the case (rare and fortuitous), then the vehicle could be on the north–south dirt road, which would lead us to Las Anod.

The driver was right. When we eventually found the road, we were virtually on the edge of the gypsum plain. To the north, I could make out the cathedral-like rocky outcrop which was Hudin, our source of fresh water. Beyond, we could see huge billowing clouds of sand sweeping across the semidesert landscape, obliterating the horizon. Now we had our bearings; within two hours we had reached our camp, near Las Anod. As darkness fell, so did the *kharif* wind.

I hope that with my digression to describe the nature of the *kharif* the reader will feel familiar with this onerous problem which affects millions who inhabit desert and semidesert areas. Now it is time to continue with my story. We are en route to Gardo.

Once we reached Gardo, Ali Nur lost no time in contacting the Locust Assistant, who told us all he knew about locusts in the area. We then drove on and, before stopping for the night, we suddenly found ourselves near a large, cultivated area. The contrast with the sandy, semidesert conditions was striking. Before our eyes were date palms, fruit trees, maize and vegetables. Soon the workers ran towards us. They explained that there had been some rainfall in the last few weeks. Now, with the hot sunshine, the crops were flourishing.

'Have you seen any locusts?' I asked.

Figure 15. Northern Somalia, 1957. Typical stony, undulating desert landscape which gradually rises to the higher elevation of the northern maritime escarpment. For long journeys, two cross-country vehicles were used, plus a back-up truck to carry fuel for the vehicles and drinking water.

Figure 16. Northern Somalia between El Gal and Durbo, 1957. Walking with burden camels in the maritime escarpment. The camels are of smaller build than desert camels, being specially bred to remain sure-footed in uneven, mountainous terrain.

'Not this year so far, but last year a huge swarm arrived. It stayed here for two weeks – and it ate absolutely everything! It was very sad; we had worked so hard for many months. Then everything was lost!'

This was the first confirmation of the presence of a large locust swarm in the general area not very far from the tip of the Horn of Africa. And if this swarm had flown so far east, without doubt others took a similar route; in its gregarious phase, the desert locust would always tend to join other swarms.

The next day we continued to press northwards. The sandy landscape gradually gave way to stony terrain, which soon became a desert of small stones and gravel. We had now entered what one might call a moonscape. The altitude was rising, and by mid-afternoon we had reached a village called El Gal. There, the villagers told us that, although a road through the mountains to the coast had been planned, construction had hardly started. So if we wished to reach the coast, we could only traverse the mountains on foot. Our belongings could be transported by camels; we could hire burden camels on the spot, which we did.

I was intrigued that camels, an animal of the desert, could be used in the stony mountains. The camel driver explained that these were specially bred for the mountains; the breed was more stocky than the camels of the desert. These animals had been trained to obey commands, usually for caution; these commands were loud and guttural. I soon learned some of the commands and the animals reacted perfectly. As these animals found their way through the maritime escarpment, I was frequently amazed how they navigated tricky, sometimes dangerous, stretches. Helped by the commands of their driver, throughout the journey they were always sure-footed.

After walking for about three hours, we decided to camp in the mountains overnight; we were now about 2,000 feet above sea level. Although we were on stony ground, there was an abundance of bushes and small trees around us.

Shortly before five o'clock on the following morning I was woken up by a heavy dew; with saturated sheets, I was encouraged to get out of bed! Now we were again on the move. After an hour or so, we reached the crest of a ridge. From there we could see the sea stretching in the early sunlight to the horizon. This was the Gulf of Aden, a southern extension of the Red Sea.

Four and a half hours later we reached a village on the coast called Durbo. For the last part of the walk the track descended very steeply; the camels, in particular, needed patient and careful guidance to prevent them from stumbling. Compared with the conditions of the previous few days, the temperature had soared to the level often found on the shores of the Red Sea; and the humidity level was uncomfortably high.

In Durbo, I soon found the resident district officer; like most Somali government officers, he was apparently new in his work. I explained the purpose of our reconnaissance and my plan to reach Cape Guardafui. The young district officer, who struck me as having great interest in what we were doing, told us all he knew about locust sightings.

But he seemed troubled with our plan to reach Cape Guardafui. He explained that the roads were so bad that it was only rarely that one could travel far, although the Italians had managed to establish a fishing school and a mini tunny fish canning factory east of Durbo. These men were invariably delivered to their place of work by sea; they would never risk trying to use a road system which was thoroughly unreliable. He personally doubted that we could reach Cape Guardafui.

The district officer gave us geographical and agricultural information about the coastal area. Some of the so-called littoral was stony and some was suitable for date production. He emphasised that this northern area felt little connection with the government in Mogadishu. And he felt the reverse was true. So, in a sense, once one reached the northern coastal area, effectively one found oneself in a different country, a country which had different values, a different lifestyle and different priorities.

I explained that we would prepare for the walk to Alula, a distance of about 50 miles. The district officer invited us to a lunch of rice and dates. Throughout, the conversation was a delight. The district officer was not only a well-educated person; he had a happy, sometimes jovial personality. Towards the end of the meal, he said,

'I have to tell you, I admire what you are doing. If one day it will be possible to control locusts, this would be a wonderful achievement. I personally have seen crops devoured; and I have seen a lot of hunger, even starvation, caused by the destruction of crops. I feel very motivated to support your efforts. So I have been thinking how I could support you. Now I have an idea. I have the use of an old Italian four-wheel drive vehicle. It's not in good condition, but if you would like to use it as you wish, you are welcome. I can also offer the services of a driver. He certainly knows his way around here. You can return the vehicle on your return. Good luck!'

An hour later we were en route to Alula. At times the coastal area was quite wide; at other times the cliffs of the maritime escarpment almost reached the sea. Apart from crossing the mouths of huge river beds, some with walls which were over 150 feet deep, we traversed date plantations.

In one area, where rocky terrain protruded almost to the shore line, I noticed rough, craggy, somewhat stunted trees rooted in black rocks; the bulbous root in the rock was an extraordinary sight. Shortly after, we saw a man holding a large, heavy dagger-like knife. With this tool he was stabbing the rough bark of one of the trees which had forced its way through a rock face. Curious, we asked him what he was doing. He explained that this was a frankincense tree.

By removing part of the bark he would have access to the tree's aromatic resin; this would soon harden.

About once a week, an Arab dhow appeared near the coastline and dropped its anchor. Those who extracted frankincense could sell their collection to the Arabs. Eventually, the frankincense would be used as a valuable ingredient of the highest quality perfumes, mainly in Europe, North America, perhaps even in Japan; or it would be burned in Christian churches throughout the world.

With this explanation, my memory took me back to a visit I had made a few years' previously to Upper Egypt. I recalled a beautifully preserved wall painting in the temple of Queen Hatshepsut, which illustrated the Egyptian boatmen bringing frankincense from the Land of Punt. And now, some 3,500 years later I was witnessing part of a similar story.

As a brief aside, after the political fragmentation, 25 or so years ago, of what was the Somali Republic of the 1960s, the self-proclaimed autonomous state in northern Somalia is today called Puntland.

About halfway to Alula, we called on the fishing school. After a few minutes the Principal appeared; he was a short, stocky man, clad only in a pair of lightweight khaki shorts. 'Be quick,' he blurted out, 'I'm a busy man. I can give you not more than five minutes. Be quick!'

'Thank you,' I responded. 'Did you ever see locusts around here?'

'Locusts? My God! Yes! About 18 months ago this whole area was invaded. I will never forget it. They blotted out the sun; can you believe that? It's true! We thought the swarm came from the direction of Arabia. But when they crossed the coast, there must have been some wind in the upper air, which blew some of the locusts back out to sea. The locusts may have been weak after their long flight. Anyway, thousands, perhaps millions, fell into the sea. The sea was yellow over a huge area; yes the sea was covered with drowned yellow

Figure 17. Egyptian wall painting, 1500 BC. The painting depicts frankincense being transported from Somalia (the Land of Punt) to Upper Egypt. Currently, the area is a self-declared State called Puntland. Export of frankincense is an important industry.

locusts. The sea became a huge yellow carpet. They made wonderful food for the tunny fish.'

The Principal looked at his watch. 'That's it,' he said, 'I'm a busy man! Goodbye.'

Our locust informant disappeared through a swing door. I was left to wonder at this dedicated man, a man who seemed to us to be working in the middle of nowhere, with his brown torso and scanty shorts, and with little time for a passerby.

We reached Alula in the afternoon and spent the rest of the afternoon and most of the following day gathering locust information. The district commissioner was a helpful person. Like most officials, he spoke Italian, but no English. Conversing in Somali, he explained that the road beyond a village called Bereda had been completely washed away. Between Bereda and Guardafui, the high ground extended to the sea. One might consider climbing, scrambling and walking to Guardafui. However, he strongly advised against this approach. With the high temperatures and the degree of exertion needed for perhaps a day and a half, physical exhaustion could not be ruled out. If the walker collapsed, little could be done to save the person.

In the circumstances, his advice was to drive to Bereda in the evening and ask the villagers for advice on how to travel further east. If the villagers were to tell us that we could not go further, then we could spend a day there to gather locust information. Then we should start our return journey.

In the evening we left for Bereda, arriving in Bereda at about midnight. To our surprise a number of villagers were awake to greet us. Although no mention had been made by the district commissioner, it seemed that a forerunner had been sent from Alula to Bereda to let the villagers know that we would be visiting them. After words of welcome and 'Peace' the Chief of the villagers spoke.

'It is our understanding that you would like to reach Guardafui. Beyond our village the road is no more. You cannot walk by the sea because of the cliffs which will bar your way. So here we have two canoes for you and we can transport you on the sea to a village called Olloch. Then, after a further short journey to Darmo you can walk to Guardafui in a few hours. If you leave here at two o'clock in the night, you should reach Olloch by about sunrise.

'I need to make one important point quite clear. You make this journey at your own risk. We use the canoes at night because the sea is usually calmer at night. But you never know. The sea can become treacherous at any time. Now don't forget that there are many sharks in the sea. So if the canoe capsizes, then it could be very dangerous. As I said, it is important that you understand what could happen.'

We left Bereda in two dug-out canoes at two o'clock in the morning. The sea was calm and above us shone a beautiful, clear moon. As I stepped into the canoe, I asked what I should do to help. One of the paddlers said,

'You are a tall man. If you move from one side to another, the canoe may capsize. That would be the end for us because in the sea we will die. Our Chief told you that. We know what we are doing. We want you to lie along the bottom of the canoe. Please lie still! We will tell you when you can move.'

I obeyed his instructions. Now we were about a hundred yards off shore and moving smoothly through the calm water. I lay still, hearing the regular strokes of the paddle. I looked at the clear moon; and perhaps I closed my eyes and dozed a little. At about five o'clock, the paddler announced that we had reached Olloch. The sea was shallow where the canoe beached, so when I left the canoe I had quite a long walk through the gentle surf.

As I reached the shoreline, it seemed that all the villagers were running towards us. Soon we found ourselves at the centre of a good number of villagers who, apparently, were curious as to why we had stopped to visit them. These were happy, laughing people, bubbling with excitement. They talked and asked questions continuously. Now one or two began to gently stroke my arms. Yes, for some this was the first time they had seen, and could even touch, a human being having skin of white pigment. What an experience for them!

After the initial burst of excitement, I began to ask questions about locusts. Of course the villagers had seen swarms from time to time. But, they explained, locusts were not their current priority. They were plagued, not by locusts, but by packs of hyenas. If I knew how to control locusts, then surely I could tell them how to control hyenas! Apologising for my lack of hyena control knowledge, we returned to the canoes.

We continued our canoe journey, with the canoe being beached at a small village called Darmo. By now the sun was well up and we could already feel its heat; from now on, it would only get hotter by the hour. The villagers directed us to walk up the hill behind their village; then we should walk in an easterly direction until the lighthouse came into view. This was Cape Guardafui.

The next 40 minutes proved to be the most exhausting walk of my life. For this period, we toiled up an extremely steep hill in soft, fine, deep sand. It seemed as though we were ascending a huge, incredibly high, sand dune. With the heat of the sun bearing down on us, we had the challenging task of making progress in the soft sand. Sometimes, strive as we might, we could make no progress at all; our feet simply sank into the sand and dragged us backwards. Then we would try again. We were doing our best, but would it be enough?

At last the ground became firmer. Although we felt extremely tired, we told ourselves we were on the crest of what was a massive hill of soft sand. In fact, the ascent equated to an altitude difference of 800 feet. As we began the walk to Guardafui, I realised my feet and ankles had been burned by the hot sand. Now the unforgettable toil was behind us. We continued walking. At the higher elevation the heat was tempered by a breeze from the seas. On our left, we were looking at the Gulf of Aden; and looking across the barren peninsula to its other side, we could see the Indian Ocean stretching to the horizon. After an hour or so, the lighthouse came into view.

A half hour later, we had reached Cape Guardafui, the tip of the Horn of Africa.

A Somali approached and shook our hands. He admitted to feeling surprised: Visitors were extremely rare, especially those on foot. He explained that the lighthouse keeper and other employees always arrived and departed by boat. I asked him if he had ever seen locusts in the area. He told us the previous year the entire sandy peninsula had been heavily infested with breeding locusts. So this meant an area of roughly ten by five miles had been infested. He said that practically all the vegetation which grew on the peninsula had been devoured.

While we were talking, the lighthouse keeper joined us. Alfredo Polidari introduced himself and welcomed us. He led us into the lighthouse and climbed a metal spiral staircase. Standing on a platform we could see the whole sandy peninsula. To our right was the Gulf of Aden, which would join the Red Sea, and on our left the Indian Ocean stretched to the horizon.

Alfredo proudly showed us the interior of the lighthouse. Most major parts were protected by highly polished brass plating. The entire mechanism struck me as well organised and everything looked in impeccable condition.

Alfredo had operated and maintained the lighthouse for two years. He lived in a small building nearby. Apart from a shed, there were no other buildings. Alfredo had a pretty, young Somali wife who looked after him and conversed in Italian. Apart from a few chickens and a row of low, staked tomatoes, the landscape was barren.

Alfredo seemed to be a thoroughly self-sufficient person. He struck me as a calm man who was contented with life. However, when I explained that we should soon start the return journey, he reacted with firmness.

Figure 18. North–eastern Somalia, 1957. The tip of the Horn of Africa – Cape Guardafui. Ali Nur, Head of the Somalia Desert Locust Control (Anti Acridica), Alfredo Polidari (Lighthouse Keeper), Colin Everard (Desert Locust Control). The base of the Cape Guardafui lighthouse is in the background.

'You mean you have come all this way to spend an hour or two with us? You don't understand! You are a rarity in this part of the world. You will stay the night. And tomorrow I will have the pleasure of serving an Englishman his English breakfast. You will stay!'

We spent the hours till dusk collecting samples of shrubs and plants, some of which I had never seen. Although my knowledge of Italian is superficial, we talked easily to one another. Alfredo was *au courant* with current affairs; for example, he was well informed on the Suez crisis.

144

After some supper, we slept well. Next morning I had hoped to depart by seven o'clock at the latest. But Alfredo had other ideas. He asked me to look around the lighthouse; he would call me as soon as breakfast was ready. After about half an hour, I heard a call; I descended to ground level and walked into a small building. Alfredo was beaming.

'Please come and sit down at the table. Here is your English breakfast.'

I sat down. The table was beautifully laid with a tablecloth of embroidered cotton. Before me was a very large omelette. In fact, it was the largest omelette I had ever seen; so, on Cape Guardafui, I experienced another 'first' in my life.

'Oh! Alfredo, this is wonderful. But you know, the omelette is huge. May I please offer you half?'

Alfredo smiled.

'I never eat breakfast! We made the omelette with 12 eggs. You are an Englishman. Please enjoy your breakfast.'

I persevered. After a few minutes Alfredo jumped up. He grabbed a matching embroidered serviette and handed it to me. He tapped his head – how forgetful!

While I was meeting the latest challenge, this time the huge omelette, Alfredo and I talked a little. I asked him about visitors. He told me that during the last two years he had received two visitors, who were together. One was a Catholic priest who, unfortunately, had suffered a heart attack. The priest died. Alfredo pointed to a grave about 100 metres away where the priest had been buried. Alfredo mentioned that he had dug the grave himself.

At the end of the sumptuous meal, it was time to leave. I was wondering about the effect of the sun on an overfed human being. Soon, with goodbyes in Somali, Italian and English, we were walking away from Cape Guardafui. After scrambling down the huge, hot hill of sand, below the peninsular, we reached Darmo. Soon we were heading back by canoe along the coast to Olloch and onwards to Bereda.

Figure 19. North–eastern Somalia, 1957. The only available method in 1957 of transportation between Cape Guardafui and Bereda, a small town near Alula, on the northern Somali coast.

Again, for stability of the canoe, I lay outstretched in the bottom of the canoe; as protection against the sun, a strip of sackcloth had been thrown over me. The return journey took less long than the paddled outward one; with the help of a fresh breeze and a sail, our canoe was towed quite swiftly through the surf. At Bereda we bade *adieu* to the villagers and reached Alula in the four-wheel drive vehicle at nightfall.

On the following day we drove to Durbo, where we returned the vehicle to the district officer. He was very interested in what we had found out about locust movements and breeding in the northern area. For our part, he received from us deep appreciation that we had had the use of the vehicle.

'I hope you didn't look underneath the old vehicle,' he said with a laugh, 'If you had, I don't think you would have risked your lives in it!'

'No,' I replied, 'We didn't look underneath – and we have arrived in one piece. So thank you again.'

As we said goodbye, the district officer mentioned that the wind would soon change from predominantly north–east to south–west, the so-called *kharif*. The *kharif* would blow for four months or so and, as it did every year, it would harm the environment, causing huge sand drifts and blowing dust and sand over vast areas. He told us the last Arab dhow of the season had left for Aden the previous evening – a sure sign that the wind was expected to change its direction.

Now we turned our attention to what lay before us. We were faced with the formidable walk up and through the mountains. Once we had reached the top of the escarpment, we would have to walk for about three and a half hours to reach the Land Rovers, which we had left at El Gal. We thought the walk through the mountains to the crest would take about four hours.

Because of the intense heat and humidity, we decided to delay the start of our walk for an hour and a half and leave Durbo at about half past two. We hoped that the temperature might cool about an hour after the start of our walk. However, the camels would walk more slowly. So they could leave with our belongings and water without waiting for us to start. Without more ado, the camels left for the walk through the mountains.

Shortly before leaving at the agreed time, a man of about 30 sat down and asked us what we were doing and where we were going. When we told him, he said;

'That's good news. I am from around here. I am also leaving for the top of the mountains. If you agree, we can go together. I have walked up there a few times. I'm lucky. I know a short cut. It's steep at first, but then it gets easier. At the top the short cut crosses the camel track. If you like, I will be your guide. Then you can wait for the camels on the ridge at the top of the mountain. And if you come with me, you won't be so tired – it's quicker!'

Turning to a youth, he added, 'This is my nephew. He is coming too.'

After talking to Ali Nur, we agreed to follow this pleasant man. Shortly after, we left. We had nothing to carry; the helper, however, carried a goatskin of water.

Our guide was right. The first hour and a half of the walk was arduous and physically challenging. Although the temperature was steadily dropping, it was still hot and the high humidity encouraged me to take off my shirt because my shirt and shorts were saturated with perspiration. The so-called short cut led us over rocks and stony ground. Sometimes the little-used track disappeared altogether. We pressed on – and up.

Suddenly, I heard a thump behind me. The helper had collapsed with exhaustion. As he fell, the goatskin of water slipped from his hand. We did what we could, which was not very much, to revive the helper. The goatskin of water had lost about three quarters of its contents. After a few minutes, the helper opened his eyes; he seemed disoriented, staring in different directions as though to recapture his bearings. After about ten minutes, Ali Nur and I supported the helper as he tried to stand up. We put his arms around our shoulders and walked slowly ahead; the helper was part carried and part dragged.

Now we had reached an altitude of 2,500 feet above sea level. We found ourselves on the ridge of a mountain. Nightfall would descend in about 45 minutes. When would we cross the main camel track? One hoped soon. Now the helper had recovered to the point where he could walk without assistance. So now our group, although feeling extremely tired, was reasonably mobile.

Suddenly, our guide stopped. He looked a changed man. He feverishly looked around as though he wanted to escape. His lips were trembling. I took his arm and asked him to tell us what had happened. Almost whispering, with short, seemingly breathless bursts of words, he announced that he had lost his way. Now he realised we were too far west. To reach the camel track, we would need to descend into the valley and work our way up the mountain to the east. The ridge on the next mountain would lead us to the camel track.

In our pitiful state of near-exhaustion, we simply glared at this man, a so-called guide who had brought us to the wrong place, a place where we found ourselves alone, and vulnerable in an inhospitable range of mountains. Of course, we were shocked. The helper broke the silence. Looking at me, he said,

'Can we kill him – now!'

Standing on that remote mountain ridge and fearful of what might happen to us, I for one could understand his outburst. In basic terms, this was a young man who felt he had been deceived and now he was becoming frightened of his possible fate. Nevertheless, no, the guide who had hopelessly misled us would not be murdered.

For our part, we found ourselves in a new, unexpected situation. First, we had separated ourselves from our water, which was somewhere being carried on a camel's back. Second, in our fatigued state, we were faced with a strenuous task, in fading light, which involved scrambling down a mountain side and climbing the next mountain to a ridge where, we hoped, we would find the main camel track. We briefly considered sleeping where we found ourselves and carrying on at dawn. But this possibility was quickly rejected. We were without water and we could not ignore the possibility that wild animals might find us. The uninhabited mountains were ideal habitats for animals such as lion and leopard.

So after our short rest, we set off again and descended the mountain side. Having reached the narrow floor of the valley rather sooner than I had expected, we prepared ourselves for the final ascent of the mountain side which towered above us. With the setting sun and with the higher altitude, I began to gain a feeling of regenerated strength.

We began the scramble up the scree which was strewn over the surface of the mountain. Gradually, the scree gave way to large stones; and shortly after, we found ourselves navigating our path through boulders. Suddenly, we were faced with a rock face which was at least 50 feet high. After traversing the mountain below the rocks, we found we could climb onto a lower rock. From our pedestal, we could progress over the higher level of the rocks. Here and there the surface of the rocks was broken, so we would either jump over the cracks, or we would need to make a detour to circumvent the gullies.

At a point where we thought we had crossed the massive rocks, I slipped in a gulley. I did not fall far, but I felt shaken; so I rested for five minutes. We then noticed that the skin had been torn from my ankle. Having tied a handkerchief around the wound, we hoped the blood would eventually congeal, which it did. We carried on, always steadily gaining altitude.

Just as dusk fell and darkness enveloped us and our surroundings, we suddenly found ourselves crossing the main camel track. After taking a few steps, we lay down on the stony ground to rest; around us I could see silhouettes of bushes and low trees. At an altitude of 3,000 feet above sea level, the air was cool and the breeze wafted gently over our weary limbs. I for one felt relieved that at last we had found the camel track.

I turned to Ali Nur.

'Well, Ali, we made it, thank goodness. It's about three hours' walking to El Gal, where the Land Rovers are. I wonder where our camels are; do you think they have already passed here?'

Before Ali Nur replied, the unmistakable sound of wooden camel bells pierced the night air. Five minutes later, the camels had arrived. We had soon cut thorny *acacia* branches to make a small zariba fence to protect us during the nocturnal hours. Then we slept.

Shortly before five o'clock the following morning, we set off for El Gal. There we transferred to the waiting Land Rovers and drove in a southerly direction to a town called

Scuscuiban. The word SCU-SCIU-BAN is an alliteration to sound like the frothing water which tumbles into a nearby water hole. Surface water north of the Shebelle river, which is in the southern part of the country, is practically unknown. Scusciuban is one of the very few exceptions.

As far as my ankle was concerned, it had become swollen and I had almost lost the use of my foot. I enquired whether there was a medical facility in the town. I was directed to a house where I could consult Dr Parisi, a medical doctor provided to Somalia by the World Health Organization. Dr Parisi, a charming and interesting man, cleaned the wound, apologising that he would unavoidably hurt me. With my foot encased in medical dressing and bandages, Dr Parisi said:

'The whole thing is a mess, I am afraid. I hope I have done enough. You won't leave my house for three days. You will stay in my bed the whole time. I will sleep on the sofa in the living room. I will decide in three days if you are fit to travel.'

Three days later, with my ankle on the mend, we drove south, reaching Mogadishu after five days of driving. There, my ankle received more medical attention; in time, it healed.

Apart from the reports which needed to be compiled, as well as sketch maps which showed likely areas for locusts' breeding, I sent 33 samples of bushes collected on our trip to the herbarium in Kenya. The accompanying list showed where and when each specimen had been found, together with its Somali name. I later received a letter to tell me that at least one of the species was new to the recorded flora of Africa.

So what had we achieved on this reconnaissance? We had clearly found out that, contrary to assumption, locust swarms moved much further eastwards at certain times of the year in the northern part of Somalia. In fact, they sometimes bred on a very large scale as far east as Cape Guardafui. Therefore we could reasonably hope that, by obtaining accurate locust information throughout the year via a locust scouting system, it should be feasible to mount campaigns to destroy locusts and their progeny in the extreme north of Somalia. By reducing the locust escape from the north, the scale of subsequent breeding in the south would be greatly reduced. Not only would agriculture and grazing be spared the destruction of ravaging swarms; the cost of mounting large-scale locust campaigns in breeding areas further south, would be much reduced.

In a nutshell, we had made yet another contribution to piecing together the complex puzzle of locust movements and likely breeding areas in the Horn of Africa.

En passant, looking back, we can hardly believe that Somalis in the twentieth century could lead peaceful lives, rarely threatened by violence. Tragically, Somalis have moved into the twenty-first century: Now, the northern part of Somalia is plagued by pirates, together with the violence which accompanies their criminal activities.

Four years later, in 1961, I made another reconnaissance in the northern part of Somalia. Instead of reaching Cape Guardafui from the towns of Alula and Bereda on the northern coast, I travelled up the eastern coast along the shore of the Indian Ocean. In addition to gathering information on possible breeding areas and so forth, I needed to verify small, but important, pieces of data compiled during my earlier reconnaissance in 1957. It was during the second reconnaissance that I investigated the presence of desert locusts in an area south of Alula; this was called the Hemistio Depression. To digress, at that time the Somali language was usually in the oral form; nowadays Hemistio would be written as *Ximistiyo*. According to local tribesmen, this was an area which harboured large and dense swarms; the north–eastern monsoon wind would eventually carry the swarms southwards, where they would breed on a vast scale.

During my reconnaissance I was surprised to learn that the word *gu* has two meanings by tribes who inhabited areas which were adjacent to one another. *Gu* usually means spring; however, at least one tribe uses the word to mean summer. When one recorded what one believed to be concrete information relating to when locusts bred in certain areas, then conflicting meanings of the same word by different Somali tribes resulted in apparent contradiction. It was surprising that adjacent tribes should interpret differently the meaning of an often-used word in the Somali vocabulary. Was this the stuff of unified nation-building? During my second reconnaissance, such confusion was clarified.

At last, I reached the lighthouse at the tip of the Horn. Alfredo embraced me. He asked me if I 'was just passing by?' I asked Alfredo how many visitors he had received since we had last met four years previously. Alfredo looked thoughtful for a moment. He looked at me, smiling just a little. Then he responded, 'One.'

7

A Change of Aircraft

In mid-1957 I was asked to assume responsibility for the protection of East Africa against invasions of desert locust swarms. The term 'East Africa' encompassed the countries of Kenya, the then Tanganyika and Uganda; the country of Tanganyika would later be renamed Tanzania after its union with the island of Zanzibar. For this work, I was based in Nairobi, the capital city of Kenya.

Historically, in the 1930s and 1940s both Kenya and the then Tanganyika had suffered disastrous agricultural damage from ravaging locust swarms. Some of the locust swarms devoured crops in Kenya. Others continued their path of destruction southwards, laying waste agricultural land in the foothills of Mount Kilimanjaro; some of the swarms continued in a southerly direction, reaching the fertile land in the Iringa area, some 400 miles south of the Kenya border.

In the 1950s, there were residents in Nairobi who could vividly recall days when huge swarms of locusts passed over Nairobi, sometimes continuously for two days. People recalled how the sun would disappear from view, with the light intensity of Nairobi being reduced to a vast gloom. The passage of these swarms had caused dislocation of everyday life in Nairobi; for example, the railway system had become paralysed as the wheels of locomotives simply spun on the rails, unable to make effective contact because of locust corpses squelching beneath them.

It would be impossible to exaggerate the negative impact of locust invasions. Since pre-biblical times, some 50 countries had suffered hunger and starvation caused by locust plagues. To offer some perspective, locust swarms of medium density extending over 400 square miles would weigh about 80,000 tons. Since, in order to survive, a locust must eat at least half of its own weight in food every day, little imagination is needed to visualise the catastrophic damage to crops and grazing which invasions of locusts could, and did, inflict.

When we talk of biblical times, this is usually a loose expression to refer to times of the distant past. We certainly know of locust plagues which wreaked havoc in Egypt some 4,000 years ago. At last, in the mid-twentieth century, primitive methods of controlling locusts were being replaced by a scientific, technical approach which promised effective control of locust plagues. By the late 1950s, the digging of trenches for locust nymphs, or hoppers to fall into, or the banging of drums or tin cans to encourage flying locusts to move on, were memories which would soon fade. Even the fielding of over 200 locust control officers, many of whom sometimes each needed to employ 200 to 300 labourers, would soon be replaced by a new, much more efficient, technological approach.

In advancing locust control methods, one of the first steps was to develop an insecticide which would kill only the locust; that is to say, the insecticide should not, under any circumstances, harm vegetation or livestock. This had already been achieved by mixing a minute percentage of a specific insecticide with bran. Now, the challenge was to convert the insecticide into a fluid. After a good deal of research and experimentation, this was successfully achieved by using a suitable fluid carrier for the minute amount of insecticide required.

Figure 20. North–eastern Kenya, 1957. A typical desert locust reconnaissance team – the driver/mechanic, two locust scouts, and the author. In the background one sees the top of an acacia *tree, the so-called 'umbrella tree'.*

Under the able direction of Philip Stephenson, several research projects had been underway for a few years. In one of these, a mechanical engineer called John Sayer had developed what was known as the Sayer Sprayer. Sayer had devised an insecticide sprayer which utilised the exhaust gases of a Land Rover. So, instead of the need to employ hundreds of labourers to spread locust bait, two or three Land Rovers would systematically traverse the terrain, spraying the vegetation with insecticide. After eating the sprayed vegetation, the locust hoppers or young adults (fledglings) would immediately die.

Another decisive step in combating the locust scourge involved aerial spraying. The effective technique to achieve this spanned several years of experimental development. When, for example, we see on our TV screens an aircraft spraying a forest fire, we give little thought to the experimentation which would have been undertaken to ensure that the dousing liquid reached its target effectively.

Most early experiments to spray locust swarms ended in failure. Initial efforts aimed to create a curtain of insecticidal spray ahead of a locust swarm. In theory, it was believed that the flying locusts' bodies would become contaminated by the insecticide and that the locusts would die. But this did not happen. Analysis showed that the wings of the adults dispersed the spray, effectively protecting the bodies of the locusts. To the surprise, and dismay, of the scientists involved in the experimental spraying, the locusts flew unscathed through the curtain of insecticidal spray.

Another aspect of the problem of aerial spraying concerned the size and weight of the spray droplet. Using a relatively small droplet size, initial experiments resulted in the spray rising and dissipating in the atmosphere, rather than descending onto the target. Experimentation to reach optimal results using the best mixture of droplet size and carrier weight took time. And what conditions were best in which to spray locusts? Eventually, it was concluded that locusts tended to be at their most dense, and therefore most vulnerable, either at dusk or in the early morning, when they were roosting.

Towards the end of the 1950s, many of the technical initiatives and consequent locust control developments, linked with our solid knowledge of locusts' migratory routes, came to fruition. When I had joined the DLC in 1952, I was told that I was one of 220 locust control field officers. These were positioned in Saudi Arabia, Oman (Wadi Hadramaut), Yemen, Eritrea, Ethiopia, Somalia, as well as in East Africa; as previously mentioned, East Africa comprised Kenya, Uganda and the then Tanganyika.

What had once seemed like an army of locust control field officers with many hundreds of labourers, together with fleets of Land Rovers and trucks, was no more. In their place, the Desert Locust Control (DLC) consisted of a core unit of one reconnaissance and three locust control spraying aircraft. The headquarters and field staff complement numbered 38.

In contrast to the locust life I had been leading in the Horn of Africa, my working life in Kenya was more regulated, in the sense that there were set working hours, with little expectation of the need for a quick reaction to combat locust activity. The reality was that by the end of 1957, anti-locust campaigns which were being conducted to the north, mainly in Ethiopia and the Somali area, were highly effective; so the aim of protecting crops and grazing to the south was being achieved.

Systematic aerial reconnaissance of north and north–east Kenya was continuous; and the locust control spraying aircraft were on stand-by, ready for action. As far as the locust threat was concerned, although the public at large in Kenya and what would soon be called Tanzania were complacent, I for one did not share this complacency. From the experience I had gained in the Horn of Africa, I recognised the potential threat of locust swarms; locusts could spring a surprise at any time and anywhere. One needed to be continuously alert and watchful.

To digress shortly, although every international civil servant needed to be seen as apolitical, in Kenya in the late 1950s it was impossible to remain totally immune to the politics of the day. The dreadful Mau Mau movement found itself in its dying days at the end of the 1950s.

Like other European dependencies at that time, a substantial plan of so-called Africanization was being implemented, and a programme culminating in national independence had been drawn up. Harold Macmillan's 'Wind of Change' was blowing across Africa. Following a planned sequence in East Africa, Kenya, the then Tanganyika and Uganda all became sovereign states in the early sixties. Naturally, at the working level the administrative infrastructure sometimes found itself under severe pressure. And locust control government departments in the East African administrations were no exception to this situation; a situation which was obviously of national concern.

Fortunately, as far as the DLC was concerned, we were well ahead with so-called Africanization. Adefris Bellehu was already functioning as the DLC liaison officer to Ethiopia, Mohamed Abdi was in charge in the Somali Republic and a talented national was in charge, in Asmara, to oversee desert locust control operations in Eritrea. There were also many knowledgeable and talented African nationals who were moving up through the system. So, unlike most other European-administered administrations, Africanization had been an on-going process within the DLC for some years.

A few years later (after I had retired from the DLC), I found myself visiting Kenya professionally as an international civil servant for a few days. En route to a courtesy call, I needed to pass through a large administrative office; some eight men and women were busy at their desks. I knocked on the door and entered. As soon as I was spotted, the eight administrative workers stood up. They eyed me in silence, apparently seized with incredulity. Then the silence was broken. A man said simply, 'We are so pleased to see you, Mr Everard. Have you come back to help us?'

My personal experience at the working level in East Africa in the late 1950s told me that racial relations were generally harmonious, with the vast majority of the population bent on making things work in the interest of the entire population.

As far as my responsibility to oversee the protection of East Africa from the locust scourge was concerned, there was never a dull moment. A good knowledge of locust activity over a huge area to the north was essential if we were to be prepared for a possible incursion into East Africa of escaping locust swarms. Systematic aerial reconnaissance would normally be expected to locate a flying swarm of locusts. But this approach would never be regarded as infallible. With changing winds, especially in the upper air, there would always be the possibility that a swarm might slip through the net of reconnaissance. And if rain had fallen in a semidesert area, then conditions for locust breeding would be ideal.

The country of Kenya stretches over some 224,000 square miles, or about 580,000 square kilometres. The geography of Kenya is diverse. The Highlands area equates to about one quarter of the country. As far as the farming industry is concerned, farming is concentrated in the Highlands of Kenya. The highest point of the Highlands is Mount Kenya; the mountain has at least three rocky peaks, each of them about 17,000 feet (a little more than 5,000 metres) above sea level. The land at the base of the mountain, as well as in the foothills, is fertile. In general, the Highlands are good farming and forestry countryside, especially for cattle rearing. However, farming success often depends on adequate rainfall. Should the rains fail, then the farmers inevitably face a severe challenge. In addition, as the land stretches at a lower altitude towards Lake Victoria to the west, large-scale tea plantations are common. Lake Victoria has an area which equates to about half the size of England. Its shores touch Kenya, Tanzania and Uganda.

To the north, north–west and east of the Kenya Highlands, the altitude of the land decreases sharply and soon one finds oneself in semidesert conditions, especially to the east and north–east; these conditions extend to the border with the Somali Republic and beyond. To the north, that is beyond Isiolo and Marsabit, a lava desert which is called the Chalbi Desert, stretches for 100 miles up to the Ethiopian border. To the north–west of Isiolo, the Turkana region is barren, the landscape strewn with volcanic lava. Here one finds Lake Turkana, which is one of the lakes of the Great Rift Valley; the Great Rift Valley stretches northwards through Ethiopia until it reaches the Red Sea. Lake Turkana, which is a little less than 300 kilometres in length, was formerly called Lake Rudolf. In the late 1800s, two men from the Austro-Hungarian Empire were the first Europeans to explore the Turkana region; they named the lake after the Habsburg Crown Prince of Austria, Rudolf.

All of the areas I have mentioned are inhabited by peoples who were law-abiding. So we were fortunate that, if we should need to undertake field work, then we could be assured of the constructive and friendly cooperation of the local people. I undertook regular visits by road to the vast country beyond the Highlands; and whether I was dealing with the Samburu, Turkana, Borana or Somali peoples, without exception my relations with these diverse tribal groups were cordial. The fact that I spoke fluent Somali was an advantage for both the Somalis and myself; in every situation, effective communication is vital. The area where locust activity was most likely to occur was to the north–east and east; this region is inhabited by Somalis.

Except for the Highlands, as explained, most of Kenya's land is some form of desert or semidesert. From a locust control point of view, we were mainly interested in the desert and semidesert. After rain, these areas would potentially prove ideal for locust breeding. At the same time, there would always be a risk that a sizeable locust swarm might be carried very rapidly on a strong wind into agricultural areas. In such a case, immediate and effective locust control measures would need to be undertaken if a disastrous loss of agricultural produce and grassland were to be prevented. Historically, when locust swarms had invaded Kenya, they tended to fly somewhat east of the Great Rift Valley. In any case, we needed to be constantly alert; with locusts, nothing could ever be taken for granted.

Although the anti-locust campaigns to the north of East Africa became increasingly effective, from time to time small swarms of locusts did find their way into Kenya. Although these swarms were usually small, perhaps covering about a square mile or so, their appearance generated reports and photographs in the press. These reports were often exaggerated and their content tended to reflect panic over the perceived threat of the widespread destruction of crops; and for the press, it was easy to accompany the reports with pictures in which the entire photograph was filled with flying locusts. One of the aims of the press is to dramatise events. For this purpose, the locust was an excellent subject.

In fact, in every case where locust swarms might appear, the swarm was easily and quickly dealt with: usually within 24 hours the locust swarm had been destroyed. Some of these small swarms managed to penetrate the agricultural area in the Highlands. When, from time to time, we visited farms to control a small locust swarm, I found the homesteads to be quite different to what I had expected. The appearance and demeanour of most farmers tended to be that of rather poor men and women who were working very hard to eke out a living. One could term their living accommodation as basic. Often, the rooms were quite small and the house roof might be of corrugated metal. On the side of the house, an elevated drum of water, supported on four poles, fed water into a shower. The furniture was mainly of wicker; often, the wicker looked seedy.

Sometimes, African or European farmers would explain that all their capital was used to invest in the farm; the quality of their living accommodation would never be a priority. Yes, somewhat in contrast to the image of farmers in the Kenya Highlands, these hardy people were working their hearts out to make a living. Their lifestyle was hard and devoid of any semblance of luxury.

I have tended to concentrate on the geography of Kenya because in the event of an invasion of East Africa by locust swarms, it was Kenya which would experience the brunt of the invasion. As far as Uganda and Tanzania were concerned, historically Uganda had suffered little from locust activity. In the case of Tanzania, however, the story was different. To the extent that a locust invasion of Kenya remained uncontrolled, then the swarms would almost certainly continue southwards. Their path of destruction would lay waste vast areas of agriculture and grassland, especially on the lower slopes of Mount Kilimanjaro.

In November of 1957 a technical application of locust control measures took place which, I believe, was of momentous historical significance in the crusade to control the scourge of the ravenous desert locust. Looking back, it seems strange that few at the time acknowledged the achievement of this landmark technical breakthrough.

One morning, sitting in my office in Nairobi, a cable appeared on my desk. This was a message from the district commissioner's office in Wajir, a Somali-inhabited town which lies not far from the border with the Somali Republic in the north–east of Kenya. The message stated that a locust scout had reported the sighting of a large swarm of locusts; the swarm had probably escaped from control measures in Somalia. The swarm was dense and it was flying in a south–westerly direction.

I immediately contacted the Airspray Unit by radio; at that time, the unit was based in Garissa, a town which lies south of Wajir and, by road, is about 300 miles east of Nairobi. About two hours later, I received word from the Airspray Unit, by radio, that a reconnaissance aircraft had located the swarm. The swarm was flying in a south–westerly direction and it measured some 35 square miles; its density was assessed as medium to dense with very dense patches. If the swarm maintained its course and flying speed, it was expected that the locusts would reach Embu, which is a town on the eastern slopes of Mount Kenya, within 20 hours. Apart from subsistence farms and market gardening, the Embu area supports intensive agriculture, especially plantations of coffee and tea.

It was agreed that I would travel to Embu and do my best to make sure that the local airstrip could be readied for the De Havilland Beaver spraying aircraft. I would need to bring with me the needed insecticide pumping gear. A supply of six 40-gallon drums of insecticide would also need to be available. I told the Airspray Unit that I would leave for Embu as soon as possible. At 6 p.m. I would aim to re-establish contact with a status report.

About an hour later, I was en route to Embu. The drive would be 130 miles and would take about four hours. I was driven in a Land Rover, while behind us followed a Dodge Power Wagon with the insecticide and pumping equipment. For most people, the drive which skirted the Great Rift Valley, with its magnificent views and beautiful woodland and flowers, would have been a glorious experience. But on this particular day, things were different; all one could think about was the impending task of combating a destructive locust swarm and how to save Embu's agriculture.

On arrival in Embu I called on the district officer and explained the ominous locust situation. A 35 square mile swarm of locusts was heading directly towards Embu. The swarm's density was medium to dense with very dense patches. So its overall weight would be about 10,000 tons. To survive, each of the millions of locusts in the swarm would need to eat at least the equivalent of half of its own weight every day; so in a nutshell, the swarm would devour some 5,000 tons of vegetation *every day*. In the case of coffee and tea bushes, if the locusts did not eat the leaves, then the locusts would almost certainly roost on the bushes. The sheer weight of the locusts would break the branches of the bushes; so the coffee and tea crop would be destroyed.

I went on to explain that we urgently needed to prepare for aerial spraying sorties, so we would need the use of a serviceable airstrip. The district officer became thoughtful, but only for a minute. Then he said, 'I understand completely. We do have a sort of airstrip, but it is not in regular use; the grass is knee high! Don't worry, in two hours the strip will be usable.'

Within 20 minutes this young administrator had set his plan in motion. The convicts of the local prison were let out, handed a sickle or similar cutting instrument, and set to work to cut the grass. Steadily, slashing to and fro, this crowd of men in their white prison shirts and trousers advanced down the airstrip. True to his word, two hours later the district officer reported that the job was finished. The airstrip was entirely ready for our use.

With the light beginning to fade, I set up the field radio. At six o'clock I was in radio contact with the Airspray Unit. I was taken aback, but not truly surprised, with the latest locust news; by now, I was conditioned to the bizarre behaviour of the desert locust. The latest news was that the reconnaissance aircraft had been shadowing the swarm for most of the day. A few hours previously the swarm had changed its flying direction. Instead of continuing on its south–westerly path, now the swarm was flying a little east of south. If the southerly flight path of the swarm were maintained, then on the next day the swarm would fly southwards, passing within a few miles of Garissa.

So if all went well, the swarm of locusts would be a perfect target for spraying sorties on the following day. However, the Airspray Unit had a logistical problem. Although the Unit had sufficient fuel for the aircraft and a good supply of insecticide, there was a relative lack of pumping equipment to fill the 100-gallon insecticide tanks which had been installed in each of the spraying aircraft. Taking this fact into account, it was agreed that the pumping gear which I had brought from Nairobi would be transferred into the Land Rover. The Dodge truck would be driven back to Nairobi.

And I, with the driver and a helper, would drive through the night to Garissa, a drive of about 350 miles. The aim was to reach the Airspray Unit in Garissa by dawn. There, we would hand over the pumping gear.

We thanked the district officer for his excellent support and, as dusk fell, we set forth for Garissa. In contrast to the highway which extended for most of the way from Nairobi to Embu, now we were faced with more than 300 miles of roads which varied between the semblance of a road to what were enlarged bush tracks. The driver explained convincingly that he knew the way to Garissa; for my part, I felt that there was no realistic option other than to accept his word. However, when we stopped from time to time, using a basic knowledge of the positions of constellations and stars, I was able to verify that we were following an easterly course.

Many of us can recall journeys which were, for one reason or another, unforgettable. The journey on which we had now embarked would become unforgettable. It is not easy to imagine, nowadays, travelling for 300 miles without seeing another vehicle. And what of the nocturnal wildlife? Our headlights often found hyena, jackals or a gazelle. Perhaps our main challenge would be how to deal with fatigue; by the time we would reach Garissa, I would have been not only awake, but exerting myself, for 24 hours.

The first six hours of the journey were, in fact, pleasant. Driving on sandy, bush roads is relatively slow; however, we were making steady progress. The driver was from the Kamba tribe and the helper was a Somali; so using a little Swahili, Somali and English, in a simple way we communicated between ourselves quite well.

It was a little after midnight when the driver announced he felt tired. We stopped in the darkness and I suggested that we should walk up and down the road to encourage our circulation to enliven us. However, our promenade was cut short; we immediately realised that a shadowy form on the road was, in fact, a hyena. Unless a hyena is hungry, the animal will not normally attack a human being. Was this animal hungry? How could we know? Something we did know, however, was that the jaws of a hyena are stronger than those of a lion. Without discussion, we returned to the Land Rover and slammed the doors shut. Just as we pulled away, there was a solid thud and the Land Rover rocked to the side. Perhaps the hyena was hungry after all! Now the three of us were very much awake!

It was not long before fatigue made itself felt again. Now we had another complication on our hands. The Somali helper convinced himself that, should we break down, at dawn we would find ourselves in the midst of a tribal area which was foreign to the Somali. He was sure he would be murdered. And because the Somali was terrified of his impending death, he began shrieking. 'Oh! Allah, Oh! Allah, save me from the devil. The devil is here. Save me! Oh! Allah!'

We stopped. I noticed he was half asleep. He seemed like a boxer who had taken a big punch; he walked a few uncertain steps, as though he was groggy. Then he lost no time in prostrating himself in the sand; as he implored the intervention of Allah, he continued shrieking.

I announced that I would drive the Land Rover until fatigue might overtake me. The driver and the helper slowly found their way back into the Land Rover. Suddenly, all was quiet. Both had instantly fallen asleep. Now we were underway again. Singing songs and reciting a little poetry, I persevered with the driving as best as I could in the darkness.

At about half past four in the morning, I realised that my level of fatigue would soon make it impossible for me to continue driving; as I drove through what had now become the eternal bush, even the bushes themselves seemed to be fuzzy; sometimes, as they appeared in the headlights they even seemed to be moving towards the Land Rover itself.

So I stopped. The driver was again awake. He announced that he felt refreshed; so he would drive and I should sleep. After a little exercise, we were ready to continue our journey. I told the driver that we should reach Garissa in about two hours. Fortunately, for the last hour or so we should be driving on the last section of the Nairobi to Garissa main road, which would be an altogether better road than the sandy tracks we had navigated up to that point; the road would have been properly constructed, with a finely compressed dirt surface. Soon we were once again underway, and I fell asleep.

Although an unbiased judgement would have agreed, I believe that I deserved some sleep; but as we know from life's experience we do not often receive what we deserve. Suddenly – and noisily – I was awoken by a loud bang; and as I opened my tired eyes, I was jerked forward. Then all was quiet in the darkness. Now I was fully awake and alert. The voice of the driver pierced the silence, 'Sorry, sir, I think I went to sleep.'

I opened the vehicle's door. In the darkness, I had the impression that the front of the Land Rover was about three feet off the ground; the front wheels were resting in a dense bush, which was about six feet high. I let myself down to the ground.

I noticed the lightening of the sky: A very faint light was gently replacing the darkness of the night, and soon it would be dawn. Looking back, in the faint light, I could see a bend in the sandy road. The driver had fallen asleep at the wheel as he approached the bend, and so had driven straight through the curve of the road. Now the Land Rover was lodged in a dense bush. We had no time to lose. Pushing the rear of the vehicle backwards, and with the driver using reverse gear to activate the rear wheels, we were soon, again, underway.

I drove for the last hour or so. With the sun already up, at six-thirty we rumbled somewhat noisily over the bridge which spans the river Tana. As we reached the far side, large, sturdy barriers of heavy wood were raised. And we finally drove into the township of Garissa.

Ten minutes later we had reached the airstrip. There, the pumping gear was offloaded. Ludwig Martel, a Polish former Battle of Britain pilot, was the senior pilot of the Airspray Unit. He explained that a reconnaissance aircraft was shadowing the swarm, which had just left its night roosting site. He expected the swarm to start passing Garissa about ten miles west of the airstrip; this would happen within the hour.

The De Havilland Beaver spraying aircraft would take off very shortly to start the systematic spraying of the swarm. They would make many spraying sorties over the next three hours or so. The wind had dropped. This would mean the swarm would be flying at about 15 miles per hour; so the target would be in range for more than three hours. The fact that additional pumping gear was now available would significantly reduce the turnaround time needed to refill the aircrafts' 100-gallon insecticide cylindrical tanks.

Ludwig Martel and I parted, each to follow a quite different agenda. Martel would organise and lead the aerial spraying effort. I would retire for something to eat, after which it would be time for a rest. Before entering a large marquee for some breakfast, I returned briefly to the Land Rover. Both the driver and the Somali helper were asleep. I gently thanked them for their efforts and told them I would make sure they would soon be offered some food. Then I mentioned to the Somali that he should be happy. The Garissa area is populated mainly by Somalis; so he should feel at home. Yes, Allah had heard his exhortations and pleas that his life should be spared at the hands of the Kamba tribe! I did not add that the Kamba are recognised as one of the most peaceful people of Kenya.

At about noon, Ludwig Martel entered the marquee. The aerial spraying operation had gone according to plan. Two last sorties were underway; the aircraft were searching for possible fragments of the 35 square miles swarm of flying locusts; if some isolated patches might be found, these would be sprayed. This would mean the virtual extinction of the swarm.

To my knowledge, this was the first time that a sizeable swarm of flying locusts had literally been sprayed out of the air.

While Martel was giving me his report, I noticed that he was accompanied by the aircraft engineer. 'Yes, Colin,' he said, 'It's funny isn't it? Whenever we have good news, too often, we have a bit of bad news as well. In one of the Beavers, the engine is leaking oil, ever so slightly. I'm here to fix it. I have taken a look at the source of the leak. It's actually within a sealed assembly; so I can't deal with it here. The aircraft will have to be flown back to the hangar in Nairobi. They will have the unit there and, of course, they have the tools and facilities to do the job properly.

'I don't anticipate any problems in getting the aircraft back to Nairobi; after all, the flight is only a couple of hours. Somebody said you've been on the go for about 30 hours. Now that the job has been done, if you like, we can give you a lift back to Nairobi. I will be up front with the pilot. Behind us is the insecticide tank. Then, right at the back towards the tail of the aircraft, there is a little bench seat. It's reasonably comfortable for a couple of hours. No problem. If you would like a lift, we will leave at two o'clock.'

The De Havilland Beaver aircraft was designed as a bush aircraft. It is a so-called short take-off and landing (STOL) aeroplane which has been used for many types of bush applications all over the world. As a passenger-carrying aircraft, it seats a pilot and five or six passengers. It can also be used to carry materials to remote locations; or it can be used for aerial spraying. This aircraft had two seats up front, while behind them an aluminium cylindrical tank had been installed; the capacity of the tank was 100 gallons. Behind the tank, there was a somewhat narrow passenger bench seat.

Figure 21. Kenya, 1960. The successful technique which was developed to destroy desert locust swarms by aerial spraying took several years to perfect. Here, a De Havilland (DHC2) Beaver aircraft is spraying locusts as they are coming in to roost.

At two o'clock we were ready to depart from the Garissa airstrip. I walked with the pilot and engineer to the waiting aircraft. The sun beat down on us from a cloudless sky; it was hot. The parched soil was dusty and crumbling beneath one's feet. I told myself that the heat should begin to subside after about an hour. We boarded the aircraft. For me, a door set in the rear of the fuselage was opened. I climbed aboard and sat on the bench; at least it was padded. The door was slammed shut. In front of my knees was the large, silvery insecticide tank; its diameter was about three feet and the tank was about four feet high. The tank would be my main view for the duration of the flight.

'Chocks away! Are you OK Colin?" I heard the pilot shout above the roar of the engine. Now we were taxiing towards the airstrip threshold. The pilot turned to line up the aircraft on the threshold. I heard the pilot giving the engine its full power. In a few seconds he would release the brake for take-off.

Then, the engine power was reduced. Mystified, I looked out of the little window. There, on the edge of the threshold, I saw two men gesticulating; I could hear that the aircraft's engine was idling. My door was opened. Above the din, I heard one man shout, 'Come out, Colin. Come out!' I obeyed: I slid through the small door and as soon as my feet touched the ground, I felt a firm hand taking my arm. I was led to a waiting Land Rover and we were driven back to the marquee. I heard the Beaver take off behind me.

Then my escort explained the situation. 'Sorry for the disruption, Colin. You must have been roasting in there. Just after you boarded, we saw a Cessna land; it belongs to the Kenya police. The pilot told us he is flying to Nairobi in half an hour. He is happy to have you as a passenger. So you should definitely travel with him. It's a twin-engined aircraft; I always like the idea of two engines because if you have an engine failure, you still have one engine. The Cessna will fly higher and faster than the Beaver, so the flight will be much more comfortable. He might even have air-conditioning.'

Again, I obeyed. The flight was uneventful and comfortable. Once we had landed in Nairobi, the pilot taxied to the DLC hangar; the duty driver stood by his Land Rover. I asked him whether the Beaver had already arrived. He said it had not. I decided I would not wait for the Beaver to land. I asked the driver to take me to Philip Stephenson's house in Limuru; this was a small township which was situated about 25 miles outside Nairobi, at about 6,000 feet above sea level. Steve, as we called him, was the director of the DLC. From his house in Limuru he was in daily radio contact with the senior field officers in the several countries where the organisation operated.

Steve was pleased to see me; and he was happy to hear my report of the destruction of the potentially ravaging swarm of locusts. Then he said, 'Colin. This is all very satisfactory. Unfortunately, we have a problem. We lost an aircraft! It just vanished. Unbelievable isn't it? At the base in Nairobi, they simply lost contact with the Beaver. They told me there's nothing out there.' Steve looked mystified; and he looked a little uncomfortably grave.

We did not have to wait long for the solution of the mystery. A report told us that there had been an aircraft accident about 100 miles east of Nairobi. The pilot and engineer had survived the accident. However, both had been injured; they were lying in a hospital some ten miles from the accident site.

Having had a somewhat strenuous 30 hours, I felt it was time for a rest.

At about noon on the following day, we left Nairobi and drove to the crash site. We had contracted two large vehicles, together with a recovery team, to recover as much as possible of the crashed Beaver. The remains would be brought to Nairobi some two days later.

Although I had witnessed crashed aircraft on two or three occasions, I believe that it is almost invariably the case that on reaching an aircraft crash site one is initially struck by shock. As one's eyes move from one part of the wreckage to the next, one becomes consumed by dismay and a feeling of helplessness. Then one's imagination kicks in. What was the degree of anxiety felt by the pilot? When did he decide an emergency landing was unavoidable – or did he leave the decision until it was too late? Were there survivors, or would one need to participate in pulling corpses from the wreckage? Eventually, one would be mentally numbed by the scene of destruction. One would stop and stare. And there was nothing to say.

There are different categories of aircraft accidents. As just one example, I recall saying *au revoir* to a pilot in Nigeria. He took off from a bush airstrip; shortly after take-off he suffered an engine failure. With little altitude, he was unable to turn and return to the airstrip. So he made an emergency landing in the bush. In case I could help in some way, I ran as fast as

I could through the bush; at last I reached the aircraft. I saw a little smoke drifting in the breeze. I rushed to the cockpit and helped the pilot get out of the aircraft. He was dazed and seemed unable to speak. I told him to run; he simply looked at me, with a blank expression. I started to pull, almost drag, him. Now he began to respond; he tried his best and started to run. Then we heard a bang behind us. We fell to the ground. I looked back. The aircraft was consumed by fire.

Compared with many types of accidents, the accident with the De Havilland Beaver had occurred in relatively straightforward circumstances. The crew had survived the accident. They had been hurt, but not killed. Due to an oil leak, there had been an emergency landing. In contrast to the flat, semidesert topography around Garissa, by the time the pilot decided to make his landing, the landscape had become undulating and stony; and there were many trees in the area. He had done his best to drop the aircraft into a clearing, but his best was not good enough. Shortly before the aircraft hit the ground, a wing had made contact with a robust tree; and the wing was severed from the fuselage. Now the aircraft lay in pieces on the ground.

My eyes took in the scene. Basically, the aircraft had broken into three sections. The wing which had been severed was virtually vertical; the end of the wing which had been joined to the fuselage, formed a base on the stony ground and the wing tip, at the other end, had come to rest high up in a tree. The fuselage had broken into two parts. The nose of the aircraft had been severely damaged and the propeller was a distorted length of metal. Then I looked at the middle and rear parts of the fuselage. The large insecticide tank was severely dented and was lying at an angle; the bright remains of the cylindrical tank looked incongruous as it partially reflected the sun's rays.

I looked at the place where I had been sitting before transferring to the police aircraft in Garissa. It was only then that I realised that what had been my seat was no more; on the aircraft's impact with the ground my seat had been destroyed in its entirety. I stared at the nothingness. Little imagination was needed to recapitulate what had happened. At the time of the crash, had I still been sitting on that little bench seat behind the tank, my death would have been, almost certainly, instantaneous and therefore, one would hope, painless.

Yes, this was yet another close call. I hoped it might be my last.

The recovery operation went well. A few days later I visited the headquarters in Nairobi of the DLC. As I passed a colleague, he stopped. Then he told me that he had heard about the Garrissa aerial spraying operation. What a success it had been!

Then he asked me what I thought of the overall locust situation and our efforts to overcome the scourge of the ravaging desert locust. I am sure that my response was more than he had bargained for. I motioned my colleague into an empty office. We sat down.

'Since you asked me a big question,' I began, 'If I may, I will give you a fairly comprehensive reply.' My questioner smiled a little; then he nodded. I went on, 'I think it is important to look at situations in context. As far as the desert locust is concerned, at least since biblical times, the scourge has caused widespread hunger, even starvation. Not only did the Egyptians, for instance, suffer from locust plagues 5,000 years ago. Many countries in Asia, the Middle East and Africa are afflicted by invasions of different species of ravaging locusts. Whereas the African Migratory and the Red Locust had been substantially brought under control, up to the mid-twentieth century it had proved impossible to control the desert locust; the desert locust affects some 50 countries.

'The reason why the desert locust could not be controlled was because this species has a separate, quite different, behavioural pattern compared with other locust species. The breeding areas of the Red and African Migratory locusts are predictable; in fact they have been mapped. These areas are usually called Outbreak Areas. So, as long as those breeding areas can be patrolled, then once breeding takes place, the nymphs can be wiped out.

'With the desert locust, however, this is not the case. Over a huge geographical area of 50 countries, breeding can take place literally anywhere and at any time; with the desert locust, there are no specific outbreak areas as such. With the desert locust, given the right environmental conditions, especially those relating to temperature and humidity, it will breed – period! Simply put, the behaviour of the desert locust is unpredictable, while with the other locusts, the opposite is the case. And it was this crucial difference that, up to the mid-twentieth century, made the problem of controlling the desert locust impossible to solve.

'When I joined the Desert Locust Control in 1952, some progress had been made in controlling locusts. Instead of banging gongs or digging trenches, a method had been developed to poison hoppers and locusts by using a carrier of bran mixed with one per cent of insecticide. This approach is still used today.

'Over the years, through mechanisation the rapid application of locust bait has led to greatly improved results. Now we have successful methods of applying insecticidal spray, not only on the ground but, as we saw in the last few days, also from the air. The ground and air combination of destroying locusts means that we can challenge and overcome the locust scourge. I am sure the present technical methodology will be refined and improved; this always happens.

'So now we have a completely new situation. For countless centuries the desert locust represented an insoluble problem. The locust ravaged vast areas of grazing and destroyed agriculture on a huge scale. Now, in the twentieth century, this problem has been overcome. Today, using our relatively recently acquired knowledge, the technical methodology is available to protect agriculture from the locust scourge.

'To just say this, sounds simple. The reality is that what, after so many centuries, has been achieved is a monumental step forward for mankind. This is especially the case for many of those in the Third World who live in poverty. The story may be unsung; but it is nevertheless a success story of incredibly far-reaching proportions. And I feel privileged to have been a small part of the story.

'In my opinion, there are two men who made crucial contributions to this success story. The first was Sir Boris Uvarov. After a great deal of painstaking experimentation in the laboratory, Uvarov published his *Grasshoppers and Locusts*. He explained his *phase theory* which, in basic terms, showed that solitary locusts could become gregarious in certain climatic conditions. So he proved that solitary grasshoppers and gregarious locusts were in fact the same insect and not, as had been believed, separate species. Through his knowledge a much greater understanding of the behaviour of locusts was revealed.

'The second major contributor is Philip Stephenson. It was his genius that directed all the diverse research projects; and he applied the results of the research to the locust control efforts we have at our disposal today. In practical terms, it was Stephenson's vision, linked with his outstanding ability to see though what he knew needed to be done, that made the control of the desert locust possible.

'Let me add one last point. In practically every success story there are sacrifices along the way. In the last few years, I have been personally acquainted with three field officers who lost their lives on the job; yes, it's very sad. A few days ago we lost an aircraft. To me, that loss seems symbolic of sacrifice. So the anti-locust story is no exception. Success is rarely achieved without sacrifice.'

My colleague gave me a long, hard look. Then he said, 'So now we have the technology and the knowledge to harness it. That's great. So what are you going to do now, Colin?' I replied, 'Well, I'm just coming up to 27. I'm going to stay for perhaps a year, maybe two. Then I'm going to move on.'

And I did.

Epilogue

Controlling the Desert Locust – the Situation in 2018. Progress and Problems

Puck: *How now, locust, whither wander you?*
Locust: *I do wander* **everywhere**

(With an apology to William Shakespeare and
his *A Midsummer Night's Dream*.)

I hope you have enjoyed what is, above all, The Desert Locust Control Story, a story from another age in a world which differed in so many ways from our world of today. My related experiences all took place in the Horn of Africa which, in the context of some 50 countries which are vulnerable to locust plagues, was a relatively limited geographical area. Having stated this, as my accounts have shown, certainly in the 1950s the Horn of Africa was an area which was repeatedly ravaged by the desert locust scourge.

Now I would like to describe the desert locust situation as one perceives it today throughout all the locust-affected countries; these countries stretch in a broad swath from West Africa, through North Africa and the Arabian peninsula to western Asia.

In addition to describing the present desert locust situation, this epilogue also serves to highlight some of the key issues which have arisen in controlling the desert locust in some 50 countries during the last 60 years.

Nowadays, research on the desert locust (*Schistocerca gregaria*) is undertaken in many universities and entomological institutions world-wide. As far as the Anti-Locust Research Centre (ALRC) was concerned, this had been established in London by the British Colonial Office in 1945.

In October 1948, with the approval of the Colonial Office, the East Africa High Commission established the Desert Locust Survey (DLS) as a department to replace the British wartime anti-locust organisations. Its role (which had a scientific emphasis) was to survey and supervise (in consultation with national anti-locust organisations, as appropriate), anti-locust activities in the Italian Trusteeship of Somalia, the British Protectorate of Somaliland, Ethiopia, Eritrea, the Aden Protectorates (including the Wadi Hadramaut), Saudi Arabia, Yemen and Oman.

In 1950 (the year in which I was first exposed to the desert locust scourge), the Desert Locust Control (DLC) was established when reports indicated that a plague was imminent. Its mandate covered the areas covered by the DLS, as well as Egypt and Sudan. In 1963, with the approaching independence of hitherto British dependencies, a replacement organisation was established, called the Desert Locust Control Organization for Eastern Africa (DLCO-EA). The DLCO-EA superseded both the DLS and DLC organisations.

Philip Stephenson had been the director of both the DLS and the DLC (Stephenson had originally been appointed as the director of only the DLS). Under his quiet, but authoritative and highly intelligent, leadership of organisations which had somewhat loose hierarchical structures, the performance of both the DLS and DLC spoke for themselves. Especially bearing in mind the diverse backgrounds of those involved in the scientific and operational work of the DLS and DLC organisations, it was a formidable achievement of Stephenson that he managed both organisations in such a way that they formed a cohesive, and very productive, whole. Mankind owes a significant debt of gratitude to Philip Stephenson.

Under the able direction of Sir Boris Uvarov, and his successor, Peter Haskell (who was fortunate to have as assistant director, Clifford Ashall, who had extensive research field experience), the ALRC performed sterling research work covering many aspects of the desert locust, especially in developing and implementing a desert locust migration forecasting system.

In 1971, the ALRC became part of a new institution, the Centre for Overseas Pest Research (COPR), with a wider brief encompassing additional pests worldwide. However, by 1979 COPR had transferred all responsibility for desert locust monitoring and forecasting to the Food and Agriculture Organization (FAO). After further institutional mergers, COPR was relocated in 1988, from London to Chatham, a town in the south–east of England in the County of Kent. By 1990, it had become part of the Natural Resources Institute (NRI); in 1996 the NRI became part of the University of Greenwich, at its Medway campus in Chatham.

As explained, the DLC was terminated in 1962. Its responsibilities were taken over principally by the FAO, which is a specialised agency of the United Nations with its headquarters in Rome; and also by the newly formed DLCO-EA. In those countries where the former (now defunct) DLC had been active, special efforts were made to increase their efficiency. In addition, desert locust-affected countries were strongly encouraged to enter cooperative agreements in facing the locust challenge.

For the information that now follows, I am indebted to Keith Cressman who generously gave of his time in directing me to documentation which tells the desert locust control story between 1962 and 2018. At the time of writing, Keith Cressman is FAO's Senior Locust Forecasting Officer who directs and operates FAO's Desert Locust Information Service (DLIS). During the last 30 years, Keith Cressman has been assessing desert locust situations, forecasting their development, and providing early desert locust warnings to the international community.

In a general sense, during the last 60 years desert locust plague conditions developed in a number of so-called Frontline countries, of which there are 21. Frontline countries (as defined by FAO) are those countries which (provided they receive rainfall) normally have desert locust seasonal breeding areas; and they almost always have solitary locust populations. The records show that plagues were experienced in several Frontline countries between 1966 and the first decade of the twenty-first century. However, most of these plagues were of limited duration, often lasting only two or three years. Except for quite short upsurges of desert locust activity along the Red Sea coastal plains in the 1990s, most plague conditions appeared in West and North African countries.

In contrast to the plagues at the end of the twentieth century and during the twenty-first century, in the 1940s and 1950s the duration and intensity of locust plagues seem to have been significantly greater. For instance, the plague period during which the author played his part in the war against the desert locust lasted some ten years.

As far as the current desert locust situation is concerned, in its monthly Desert Locust Bulletin (which is available globally on *Locust Watch*), FAO describes the locust situation in mid-2018 as 'calm and non-threatening'.

As explained, a huge amount of desert locust research and consequent development of desert locust control methodology has occurred during the last 60 years. This has been closely linked to technological advances. So with the parallel development of, for instance, electronics, satellite technology and potential biological (as opposed to chemical) approaches, the tools now used to fight the war against the desert locust have taken a quantum leap forward, and to good effect for mankind.

In his paper entitled 'Role of remote sensing in desert locust early warning' (*Journal of Applied Remote Sensing*, 2013), Keith Cressman explains the current strategy which is used in controlling the desert locust scourge. He writes:

Locust-affected countries and the Food and Agriculture Organization (FAO) of the United Nations have adopted a preventive control strategy to manage desert locust infestations. This strategy relies on early warning and early reaction; that is, to constantly monitor desert locust breeding habitats by carrying out ground surveys on a regular basis, identifying desert locust infestations that require treatment, and undertaking control operations before the hoppers become gregarious and form hopper bands and adult swarms that can lead to an outbreak.

So how does this strategy function on a day-to-day basis? In order to understand this, it is necessary to explain briefly the main elements of the detection and forecasting system.

The area of the 21 Frontline countries equates to approximately 16 million square kilometres. In terms of the habitat of the desert locust, this area needs to be kept under constant surveillance. Much of the area is desert and locust populations rely for their food on the sparse annual vegetation that survives in semidesert conditions, supplemented by ephemeral growth of vegetation, which appears after seasonal rainfall.

As for the desert locust populations, the locusts that inhabit these areas are usually in the solitary state; I have explained the outline of the phase theory (both solitary and gregarious) in Chapter 3 – The Locust Life, as well as at the end of Chapter 7 – A Change of Aircraft.

Surveillance of this vast, often uninhabited, area has been revolutionised by the introduction of satellite technology. A satellite can not only transmit images of the area under surveillance, but areas of green vegetation can be identified in detail.

In Chapter 2 I have related how Somali Elders associated the arrival of locust swarms with rainfall and consequent growth of good grazing, which was beneficial for their livestock. Now, 60 years later, satellite pictures are confirming the correctness of the Somali Elders' statement.

Every locust-affected country maintains an operational desert locust control unit. Apart from their primary task of controlling locust hoppers and locust swarms, these units not only carry out regular reconnaissance of potential locust breeding areas, but are also constantly ready for action.

Before we come to the critical coordination of the elements which now exist to fight the desert locust, one needs to understand the basic behaviour of the desert locust, whether in its solitary or gregarious phase.

Within the vast area of 16 million square kilometres where desert locust populations exist, unless the locusts have already, undetected, changed from the solitary to the gregarious state, the desert locust populations are harmless. Now we have to take into account a crucially important behavioural factor.

When solitary desert locusts become gregarious, the transformation period is not abrupt. The locust moves through the transformation phase during two, three, or more generations. This transient stage was once scientifically referred to as a *transiens* phase, but is now best thought of as being a halfway-house between the solitary and gregarious extremes and is sub-divided into congregating transients and segregating transients for insects at the respective initiation and termination of gregarious behaviour. When watching the behaviour of a desert locust in the transient stage, and after taking some standard measurements of samples, a trained and experienced eye is needed to make an approximate assessment of the remaining period before the locust reaches the gregarious phase.

This knowledge is crucial in terms of controlling potential desert locust outbreaks. The all-important element of *time* (typically nine months, more or less, depending when the transient locusts will have been discovered) comes into play. Time is therefore given to put in place the essential control measures. As soon as the gregarious adult locusts are ready to breed, the fully prepared desert locust control units can, without further delay, deliver a knock-out blow which, in consequence, prevents an outbreak from developing.

The nerve centre of the desert locust world which co-ordinates the various elements I have described is situated at the headquarters of FAO in Rome, Italy. There, Keith Cressman and his colleagues ensure that FAO's Desert Locust Information Service, together with the Desert Locust Early Warning System, function at the optimum level. With satellite imagery, complex computer modelling based on reports of desert locust movements, changes in ecological conditions, weather data and so forth, the Service has functioned on a 24-hour basis throughout the year since 1978; and improvements in its functioning are considered, and effected as warranted, on a continuing basis. With the help of this service countries throughout the 16 million square kilometre area, and as necessary beyond, are advised of probable locust breeding areas which need immediate investigation. For their part, desert locust control units can feed desert locust information into the system using hand-held rugged mobile tablets equipped with Global Positioning System (GPS) that transmit data in a matter of seconds via satellite.

Now that we know what is being done, around the clock, to combat the desert locust, we can well visualise a desert locust scout standing in a remote desert, or semidesert, part of the world; such a place is either uninhabited or rarely visited for grazing after seasonal rain. Perhaps after travelling for two or three days, at last the scout reaches a large stretch of fresh, green ephemeral vegetation; the vegetation has taken root after recent rainfall.

The desert locust scout has been sent there by his desert locust control unit because his unit has been advised of the green vegetation satellite images which have been observed by FAO. The scout has been trained in all aspects of desert locust control, either on-the-job or possibly through a fellowship training scheme which has been arranged and funded by FAO. Patrolling the green vegetation, suddenly the scout sees locust nymphs or hoppers, which are concentrating and starting to form small but dense groups. From the behaviour of the hoppers, he realises that they are starting to become gregarious and could form well-organised ravenous and marching bands.

Armed with his GPS instrument he reports what he has found back to his headquarters, and to FAO in Rome; to do this he uses a tablet specially programmed for desert locust reporting. Within a day or two, the strategy of controlling the hoppers is put into action; the hoppers are destroyed. So at least from this area, a remote area of desert or semi-desert, there will be no outbreak of flying, ravenous desert locust swarms.

In cases where a desert locust control unit is stretched beyond its capacity in fighting a potential large-scale desert locust outbreak, at the request of the government concerned, FAO will do its utmost to seek donor support to strengthen the efforts in the affected country.

When one learns of current anti-locust technology, one could be tempted to compare the technology of today with that of years gone by, for instance in respect of the time needed to transmit a message. In the nineteenth century, an Englishman called General Kitchener sent his famous message from the Indian subcontinent to Queen Victoria in England: 'I have Sind.' Queen Victoria received her General's message three months later. In the mid-twentieth century (before the advent of the computer age, including the internet), Morse code communication was superseded by voice communication, as well as the cable, the telex and so forth. Now, in the twenty-first century, there are remarkable advances on so many technological fronts, of which communications is but one. As for future utilisation of sophisticated technology to fight the desert locust, the use of drones is just one in an array of possibilities.

In September 2017, Keith Cressman summarised the present crucially important role of FAO in participating in the war against the desert locust. Here I would like to quote pertinent parts of his summary. The information he provided reflects the strategy which has been approved by FAO's Commission For Controlling The Desert Locust.

> 1. FAO operates a global desert locust early warning system that monitors weather, ecological conditions and the desert locust situation on a 24 hours, seven days a week basis, using the latest technologies in communications, remote sensing and data collection, management, and spatial analysis. The system is operated by FAO's Desert Locust Information Service (DLIS) based at FAO headquarters in Rome. Since 1978, DLIS continues to produce and disseminate a monthly Desert Locust Bulletin that summarises the current situation and presents a 6-week forecast for each of the Frontline countries affected by the desert locust. DLIS also develops new tools and methodologies for monitoring and early warning.
>
> 2. The early warning system is the primary component of the preventive control strategy adopted by affected countries and FAO to reduce the frequency, duration

and intensity of devastating plagues. It relies on timely and regular field surveys undertaken by national locust units and the exchange of information in real time by all countries through a collaborative network.

3. FAO also strengthens national capacities in (a) monitoring of Desert Locust breeding areas, (b) rapid response to outbreaks, (c) well-developed contingency plans for emergencies, (d) training of national staff, and (e) safe and effective control measures including bio-pesticides. It is the responsibility of each affected country to monitor its territory and conduct the necessary control operations.

4. During desert locust emergencies such as upsurges and plagues, FAO solicits donor assistance on behalf of the affected countries and assists in the organisation of large-scale ground and aerial control campaigns.

5. In the last 20 years, there have been improvements in spray equipment and the use of the Geographic Information System (GIS), so that contact pesticide can be applied more effectively and the sprayed areas are better defined. A fungus biopesticide, called 'Green Muscle', has been developed and is commercially available as an option (or supplement but probably not a substitute) to be used instead of conventional pesticides, especially for use in environmentally sensitive areas. In addition, there have been substantial and significant developments in communications such that each team uses a handheld tablet to record survey and control data in the field; this is sent in real time by satellite to the national locust control centre in the respective country as well as to FAO. This means that at any given moment, we know precisely where the teams and locusts are in the field.

When I was professionally active, sometimes I used to remark to my colleagues that if we could *really* (as opposed to superficially) understand a problem, then we should be well on the way to solving it. Yes, in terms of understanding the behaviour of the desert locust and applying effective control measures, a great deal of progress has been achieved in the last 60 years.

Up to this point I have described the progress which has been made in controlling the desert locust. In order to complete the picture, now we have to learn of the current problems which prevent us from achieving complete desert locust control, thus bringing devastating locust plagues finally to an end.

A major general problem which impedes practical progress in controlling desert locusts is the fact that many (about two-thirds) of locust-affected countries are so-called Third World countries; some of these are designated by the United Nations as *Least Developed Countries* (LDCs). Third World countries are those which find themselves in some stage of development in comparison with countries of the so-called developed world. This fact has a direct bearing on the capability of both *Frontline* and *Invasion* countries to cope with desert locust plagues.

The way in which many of the challenges faced by Third World countries is managed, often strongly differs to the course of action which would probably be adopted by developed countries in a similar situation. Whereas a developed country has at its disposal a solid, experienced infrastructure, this is frequently not the case in a developing country. And whereas a developed country has ready access to funding to support important projects, too often a Third World country finds itself in a parlous state, especially when it comes to necessary foreign exchange (hard currency) to purchase equipment or services.

To offer a specific example of the type of problem which may need to be faced by a Third World country, the capital cost of buying aerial spraying aircraft would certainly be a high financial component of a hard-pressed budget, as would be the cost of the maintenance of the aircraft; in addition, the cost of the salaries of the crew members would need to be financed.

In the context of combating desert locust plagues, every affected country accepts its responsibility to put in place the human and physical infrastructure needed. However, within the country concerned, such a project has to compete for funding with, for example, measures to alleviate poverty, improved education, the provision of medical facilities, and so forth. So the challenge of actually realising effective desert locust control is a factor that must be properly considered. Certainly, the international community has a very important role to play in supporting countries' efforts to control desert locust plagues. Without essential international support, an unchecked desert locust plague will, inevitably, result in dire consequences for the country concerned. These consequences will involve destruction of crops and grazing, leading to widespread hunger and starvation.

We live in a dangerous world. If the present tempo of conflict between the more powerful nations persists, our world may eventually find itself on the irreversible road to implosion. Mankind, currently at war with itself, has always suffered from aggressive competition; and our world of today is plagued with conflict, wars, terrorism of one sort or another, civil strife and suspicion at every turn. So in the context of controlling desert locusts, thus avoiding widespread famine (sometimes starvation), there are important areas in Frontline countries which are simply off limits, in terms of controlling desert locust plagues.

For instance, at the end of Chapter 6, I have related that the Hemistio (Ximistiyo) Depression in north–eastern Somalia, which is south of Alula, sometimes harbours dense concentrations of desert locust swarms. But who would venture there today? The whole area around Alula (in what is currently called Puntland) is infested with pirates; they revel in kidnapping and physical violence, including murder.

In the context of aerial spraying of desert locust swarms (as described in Chapter 7), it is a sad reflection of our troubled world that if, for instance, it is decided to transfer a locust spraying aircraft from one country to another, apart from delays encountered in gaining clearance from the (often suspicious) recipient country, it may well be either impossible to obtain insurance cover for the aircraft, or the insurance cost involved is prohibitively high, due to the perceived high risk element of danger involving the aircraft and its crew. Ravenous locust swarms, which may be covering up to 150 miles per day, are approaching cultivated areas. But the option of using locust spraying aircraft is nullified; insurance cost and bureaucratic clearance hurdles prevent speedy and effective defense. Yes, desert locust swarms have no respect for borders and they move fast. So delays in putting in place defense measures may lead to catastrophic damage to agriculture and livestock grazing.

If we take into account what I have explained in relation to many locust-affected countries, unless the overriding and far-reaching political problems of our world can be resolved, then the achievement of complete desert locust control will remain an elusive goal. Unfortunately, without peace in our world, technological progress on its own will never be enough to solve the terribly devastating problem of desert locust plagues. We need to make corresponding advances in our civilisation.

As always, however, hope springs eternal – and so it should be!

Afterword

I n the spring of 2016, after I had drafted this book,
I found myself reflecting on danger. In all of my related
accounts, a common element recurs, namely, circumstances of danger. How do we perceive danger? Depending
on our nature, the response seems to cover a wide spectrum
of attitudes.

What follows is the final section of this book. Now I would
like to offer some thoughts on perceptions of danger. I am
excluding those in the military because, by definition, a
member of the military inevitably accepts the challenge of
danger. As a young man I served in the army. Even though
I undertook my service by conscription, I nevertheless
accepted the challenge of danger; my inner self told me there
was no alternative.

When I left the DLC I was 31 years of age. I received
a letter of appreciation from the Director of the DLC,
Philip Stephenson. In his letter, Stephenson wrote; 'The
task in the field was hard, at times very hard, and even
dangerous...' He was right. But as a young man I had given
hardly a thought to the danger element. However worthy
the endeavour might be, to some the analogy might spring to
mind that, like fools, young men often 'rush in where angels
fear to tread'.

In our daily lives we routinely watch those who function professionally in a potential danger zone. In today's nuclear and electronic world, the danger element is frequently apparent. To cite a straightforward example, the captain of a large transport aircraft who takes the responsibility for the lives of, perhaps, 300 passengers, makes hundreds of take-offs and landings during his or her professional career, a career which may include several thousand hours of flying experience. In many functions of flight, there is a potential for catastrophic danger. Yet, the danger inherent in flying is virtually nullified. Why? Because the required technological competence, linked with experience, negates the danger element. And it is interesting to note that a significant minority of travellers perceive danger in flying even though, of all forms of transportation, statistically, flying is *by far* the safest form of transportation.

Often, the older one becomes, the greater the likelihood that one would opt to avoid perceived danger. If, for instance, I might be invited to return to the Somali area, I would surely hesitate; with maturing years, and in contrast to the attitude I adopted as a young man, my perception of the current danger element would hold me back. Yet, for others this is not the case; travel firms offer several group visits each year to both Hargeisa and Mogadishu, so that tourists can enjoy not only Somali culture, but also the sun, the sand and the clear, warm waters of the Gulf of Aden or the Indian Ocean. Again, we have wide differences in perceptions of danger.

Our perceptions of danger are not limited to what might be termed the tangible. In our day-to-day living, although the perceived danger of nuclear proliferation is less tangible, nevertheless in basic terms many of us perceive nuclear activity as dangerous. Again, although few under-stand the technology of intercontinental ballistic missiles, the image of these terrifying, armed missiles creates a perception of danger.

Many perceive international terrorism as a highly dangerous threat to our very existence. In fact, there are those who perceive the world generally as a dangerous place in which to live and work. Especially among older people who have observed during their lives the development of devastatingly dangerous weaponry, there may well be a tendency to perceive the world, as we know it, to be degenerating inexorably towards extinction through large-scale destruction of humankind.

To reinforce the general perception of danger, there are many who are thoroughly discouraged by widespread, low-quality political leadership. Too many political leaders are amoral and corrupt. When this occurs in the more powerful countries of the world, many perceive resultant danger in the situation.

The unknown merits a mention in the context of perceived danger. Many of us are at best uncomfortable with the unknown; and, depending on the associated circumstances, we may well convince ourselves that we are looking at a dangerous situation.

Among the younger members of the population, there are those who are attracted by the adventure element in the unknown and any perceived danger is brushed aside. We all know that, in a wider sense, man has historically prospered by delving into the unknown. But those who did so did not represent the majority; they were often uniquely the exception to the general rule. Our world will always need a Sir Edmund Hillary, or those who explore outer space.

So how do we perceive danger? Most of us prefer not to dwell on the subject. After the experiences I have related in this book, one might ask how I perceive danger. My response would borrow a phrase used by authors and poets through the ages – in many situations danger, like beauty, is in the eye of the beholder.

Dear Reader – Adieu!

Appendix

A List of Countries Affected by Desert Locust Plagues Classified by the Food and Agriculture Organization (FAO) as *Frontline* or *Invasion* Countries

FRONTLINE (21)

Note: *Frontline* countries are those where seasonal conditions exist on a continuing basis for desert locusts to breed. These countries usually support populations of desert locusts which are solitary in behaviour. However in certain ecological conditions, the solitary desert locusts may become transient and change their behaviour into the gregarious phase. Once this happens, the desert locust breeding areas become potential outbreak areas, from which, unless they are immediately controlled, gregarious swarms will escape. This situation will create a desert locust plague.

Algeria
Chad
Djibouti
Egypt
Eritrea
Ethiopia

India
Iran
Libya
Mali
Mauritania
Morocco (and Western Sahara)
Niger
Oman
Pakistan
Saudi Arabia
Senegal
Somalia
Sudan
Tunisia
Yemen

INVASION countries are shown on the following page.

INVASION (29)

Note: *Invasion* countries are those where solitary locusts are not usually found; also, normally they do not have desert locust breeding conditions. However, during desert locust plagues they may well be invaded (as related in the cases of Kenya and the present-day Tanzania, in Chapter 7).

Afghanistan
Bahrain
Benin
Burkina Faso
Cameroon
Cape Verde
Gambia
Ghana
Guinea
Guinea-Bissau
Iraq
Israel
Ivory Coast
Jordan
Kenya
Kuwait
Lebanon
Liberia
Nigeria
Palestine
Qatar
Sierra Leone
South Sudan
Syria
Tanzania
Togo
Turkey
Uganda
United Arab Emirates

Index

www.ingramcontent.com/pod-product-compliance
Ingram Content Group UK Ltd.
Pitfield, Milton Keynes, MK11 3LW, UK
UKHW020733280225
455688UK00012B/641